50 WALKS IN THE
Peak District

50 Walks in the Peak District

Published by AA Publishing (a trading name of AA Media Limited, whose registered office is Grove House, Lutyens Close, Lychpit, Basingstoke, Hampshire RG24 8AG; registered number 06112600)

© AA Media Limited 2023
Fifth edition
First edition published 2001

Mapping in this book is derived from the following products:
OS Landranger 109 (walk 19)
OS Landranger 110 (walks 1-18)
OS Landranger 118 (walks 21, 28-29, 35)
OS Landranger 119 (walks 20, 22-27, 30-34, 36-48)
OS Landranger 128 (walks 49-50)

© Crown copyright and database rights 2023 Ordnance Survey. 100021153.

Maps contain data available from openstreetmap.org © under the Open Database License found at opendatacommons.org

ISBN: 978-0-7495-8326-2
ISBN: 978-0-7495-8353-8 (SS)

A CIP catalogue record for this book is available from the British Library.

AA Media would like to thank the following contributors in the preparation of this guide:
Clare Ashton, Tracey Freestone, Lauren Havelock, Nicky Hillenbrand, Ian Little, Richard Marchi, Nigel Phillips and Victoria Samways.

Cover design by berkshire design company.

Printed by Stamperia Artistica Nazionale - Trofarello - TORINO - Italy

A05836

We would like to thank the following photographers, companies and picture libraries for their assistance in the preparation of this book. Abbreviations for the picture credits are as follows:
Alamy = Alamy Stock Photo
Trade cover: Daniel Kay/Alamy
Special sales cover: Frank Fell/Alamy
Back cover advert clockwise from bottom left: courtesy of The Plough, Lupton; SolStock/iStock; AA; EmirMemedovski/iStock
Inside: 12/13 Andrew Kearton/Alamy; 29 Andrew Kearton/Alamy; 39 steven gillis hd9 imaging/Alamy; 49 Loop Images Ltd/Alamy; 59 Paul Richardson/Alamy; 69 Matt Gibson/Alamy; 85 NorthScape/Alamy; 101 Loop Images Ltd/Alamy; 117 Dave Porter/Alamy; 133 Rollo2019/ Stockimo/Alamy; 149 Neil McAllister/Alamy; 159 Frank Fell/Alamy; 169 Harvey Wood/Alamy

Discover AA-rated places to stay and eat at www.ratedtrips.com

AA

50 WALKS IN THE
Peak District

CONTENTS

The walks

HOW TO USE THIS BOOK

Each walk starts with an information panel giving all the information you will need about the walk at a glance, including its relative difficulty, distance and total amount of ascent. Difficulty levels and gradients are as follows:

Difficulty of walk
● Easy

● Intermediate

● Hard

Gradient
▲ Some slopes

▲▲ Some steep slopes

▲▲▲ Several very steep slopes

Maps
Every walk has its own route map. We also suggest a relevant Ordnance Survey map to take with you, allowing you to view the area in more detail. The time suggested is the minimum for reasonably fit walkers and doesn't allow for stops.

Route map legend

- -▶- -	Walk route	▢	Built-up area
❶	Route waypoint	▢	Woodland area
- - - -	Adjoining path	🚻	Toilet
●	Place of interest	P	Car park
⌂	Steep section	⊞	Picnic area
\\\|//	Viewpoint	)(	Bridge
ⅢⅢⅢⅢⅢⅢ	Embankment		

Start points
The start of each walk is given as a six-figure grid reference prefixed by two letters referring to a 100km square of the National Grid. More information on grid references can be found on most OS Walker's Maps.

Dogs
We have tried to give dog owners useful advice about how dog friendly each walk is. Please respect other countryside users. Keep your dog under control, especially around livestock, and obey local bylaws and other dog control notices.

Car parking

Many of the car parks suggested are public, but occasionally you may have to park on the roadside or in a lay-by. Please be considerate about where you leave your car, ensuring that you are not on private property or access roads, and that gates are not blocked and other vehicles can pass safely.

Walks locator map

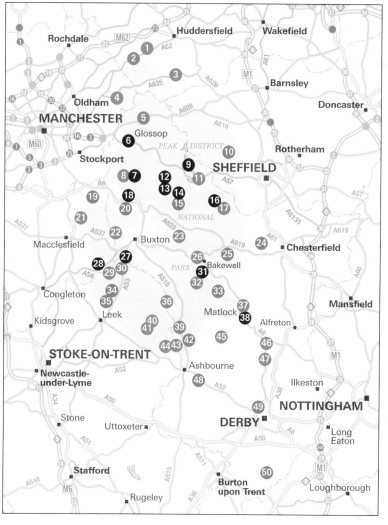

EXPLORING THE AREA

The Peak District sits at the base of the Pennines, with one foot in the North and one in the Midlands. At its northern tip, the high moorlands merge seemlessly into the South Pennine massif dividing Yorkshire and Lancashire. In the south, the graceful River Dove flows out of the limestone landscape, dividing Derbyshire and Staffordshire. Between these two contrasting images lies the Peak District National Park. The Peak District National Park was the first National Park to be established in England in 1951 and protects 542sq miles (1,404sq km) of this precious environment.

Plateau

Despite the name, you shouldn't expect to find any mountain peaks in this beautiful upland. The name comes from the Old English 'peac', which describes a knoll or hill. With a few notable exceptions, the heights are predominantly plateau-like, carved with deep valleys that give a sense of elevation to the various edges and occasional summits bold enough to lift their contours above the rest. Best-loved among these are the conical elevations of Shutlingsloe, Shining Tor, Chrome Hill and Parkhouse Hill.

Dark Peak

The northern area is known as the Dark Peak. It's one of brooding moorlands, green valleys and many reservoirs. From the gritstone outcrops and peaty morasses tumble well-fed streams. The abundance of water drew the industrialists of the surrounding conurbations, and virtually all the valleys except Edale boast a reservoir, or often several. You'll see this as you walk around the moorland fringes of West and South Yorkshire, in the Holme Valley and around Bradfield. From Glossop, Hayfield, Longdendale and Chinley on the western side each valley seems to have been dammed in turn. The most dramatic is the upper Derwent Valley, where villages were removed and vast acres of poor farmland flooded to make a series of breathtaking waterscapes. With its tales of mass trespass and pioneering access agreements, this is the heartland of the English rambling tradition. However, the walking here can be harder than it is in the limestone dales to the south. The weather can quickly take a dramatic turn for the worse, even on a sunny day, and navigation can become more problematic as the moors are engulfed in impenetrable cloud. The highest points of Kinder and Bleaklow surpass 2,000ft (610m) and heavy snowfall is not uncommon in the winter months.

White Peak

Gentler walking can be found in the southern half of the district. The White Peak takes its name from the limestone that dominates the scenery. Here you will find tiny valleys carved into the plateau – Lathkill Dale, Monsal Dale, Mill Dale and Wolfscote Dale. Perhaps the most famous is Dovedale, chaperoning the River Dove through a landscape of bizarre rock pinnacles and caves steeped in mythology. The River Manifold, too, cuts a dramatic gorge, flanked by limestone crags and mysterious chasms. You'll find many pretty villages here as well – Tissington, Hartington, Youlgreave and Ashford-in-the-Water – fine places to grab a quick bite. The Derwent Valley momentarily opens out, south of Baslow, making space for the parklands surrounding Chatsworth House. Here, the Duke of Devonshire's palatial home sits in a splendid green vale, with gritstone edges to the east and limestone dales to the west.

Gritstone fringe

Fingers of gritstone surround the White Peak, giving Cheshire and Staffordshire a moorland fringe. From Crich Stand the defiant heights look out over much plainer territory. You can follow a gritstone trail along the serene edges overlooking Bollington and Macclesfield, or linger around the shores of Tittesworth Reservoir, or the rocky towers of the Roaches.

Industrial relics

Industry has always tried to tame this landscape, but somehow the remains of the mills, lead mines, quarries and railways have blended in to add to its romance. Certainly the easy access afforded to walkers by trails on former railway trackbeds has added greatly to the Peak District's charm. Where steam trains once wound their course through Monsal Dale or across the limestone plateau, so the modern walker can now stride in confidence on the Tissington, High Peak and Monsal trails. Before the railways it was the 'Jaggers' with their trains of packhorses who crossed these hills. Now you can follow their routes over high moors and through lonely dale heads. They carried salt and coal through this beautiful landscape long before anyone considered it to be one worth preserving.

Beyond the National Park

Beyond the National Park, the Midland plain reaches up to capture the towns and villages of South Derbyshire. Here you will find a very different walking experience, in the parkland of great houses such as Melbourne, Markeaton, Osmaston, Shirley and Calke Abbey. But don't overlook it. The character of the landscape may be very different from that of the Peak District proper, but for many its warm brick-built buildings will provide a welcome contrast to the ubiquitous stone of its northern neighbours.

Snapshot

These 50 walks represent a snapshot of the opportunities available to those prepared to muddy their feet and stray off the beaten path. From high points to low, light to dark, you'll find the Peak District has a lot more to offer the walker than tea shops and show caves, and hopefully the walks in this book will inspire you to return to the many delights of the area again and again.

WALKING IN SAFETY

All these walks are suitable for any reasonably fit person, but less experienced walkers should try the easier walks first. Route-finding is usually straightforward, but you will find that an Ordnance Survey walking map is a useful addition to the route maps and descriptions; recommendations can be found in the information panels.

Risks

Although each walk here has been researched with a view to minimising the risks to the walkers who follow its route, no walk in the countryside can be considered to be completely free from risk. Walking in the outdoors will always require a degree of common sense and judgement to ensure that it is as safe as possible.

- Be particularly careful on cliff paths and in upland terrain, where the consequences of a slip can be very serious.

- Remember to check tidal conditions before walking on the seashore.

- Some sections of route are by, or cross, busy roads. Take care, and remember that traffic is a danger even on minor country lanes.

- Be careful around farmyard machinery and livestock, especially if you have children with you.

- Be aware of the consequences of changes in the weather, and check the forecast before you set out. Carry spare clothing and a torch if you are walking in the winter months. Remember that the weather can change very quickly at any time of the year, and in moorland and heathland areas, mist and fog can make route-finding much harder. Don't set out in these conditions unless you are confident of your navigation skills in poor visibility.

- In summer remember to take account of the heat and sun; wear a hat and carry water.

- On walks away from centres of population you should carry a whistle and survival bag. If you do have an accident that means you require help from the emergency services, make a note of your position as accurately as possible and dial 999.

Countryside Code
Respect other people:

- Consider the local community and other people enjoying the outdoors.

- Co-operate with people at work in the countryside. For example, keep out of the way when farm animals are being gathered or moved, and follow directions from the farmer.

- Don't block gateways, driveways or other paths with your vehicle.
- Leave gates and property as you find them, and follow paths unless wider access is available, such as on open country or registered common land (known as 'open access land').
- Leave machinery and farm animals alone – don't interfere with animals, even if you think they're in distress. Try to alert the farmer instead.
- Use gates, stiles or gaps in field boundaries if you can – climbing over walls, hedges and fences can damage them and increase the risk of farm animals escaping.
- Our heritage matters to all of us – be careful not to disturb ruins and historic sites.

Protect the natural environment:
- Take your litter home. Litter and leftover food don't just spoil the beauty of the countryside; they can be dangerous to wildlife and farm animals. Dropping litter and dumping rubbish are criminal offences.
- Leave no trace of your visit, and take special care not to damage, destroy or remove features such as rocks, plants and trees.
- Keep dogs under effective control, making sure they are not a danger or nuisance to farm animals, horses, wildlife or other people.
- If cattle or horses chase you and your dog, it is safer to let your dog off the lead – don't risk getting hurt by trying to protect it. Your dog will be much safer if you let it run away from a farm animal in these circumstances, and so will you.
- Everyone knows how unpleasant dog mess is and it can cause infections, so always clean up after your dog and get rid of the mess responsibly – bag it and bin it.
- Fires can be as devastating to wildlife and habitats as they are to people and property – so be careful with naked flames and cigarettes at any time of the year.

Enjoy the outdoors:
- Plan ahead and be prepared for natural hazards, changes in weather and other events.
- Wild animals, farm animals and horses can behave unpredictably if you get too close, especially if they're with their young – so give them plenty of space.
- Follow advice and local signs.

For more information visit www.gov.uk/government/publications/the-countryside-code

ALONG THE COLNE VALLEY

DISTANCE/TIME	7 miles (11.3km) / 4hrs
ASCENT/GRADIENT	1,000ft (305m) / ▲ ▲
PATHS	Field paths, good tracks and canal towpath, many stiles
LANDSCAPE	Typical South Pennine rough pastures, canalside
SUGGESTED MAP	OS Explorer OL21 South Pennines
START/FINISH	Grid reference: SE079140
DOG FRIENDLINESS	Towpath is especially good for dogs
PARKING	Plenty of street parking in Slaithwaite, free car park near the library
PUBLIC TOILETS	Marsden

Transport across the Pennine watershed has always presented problems. The Leeds and Liverpool Canal, built during the 1770s, took a convoluted route across the Pennines, through the Aire Gap at Skipton. Then came the Rochdale Canal. However, its more direct route came at a high price: mile for mile, this canal has more locks than any other inland waterway in the country. With the increase in trade between Yorkshire and Lancashire, a third route across the Pennines was soon needed. The Huddersfield Narrow Canal links Huddersfield with Ashton-under-Lyne in Greater Manchester. Though only 20 miles (32.2km) long, it includes the Standedge Tunnel. Begun in 1794, and dug with pick, shovel and dynamite, the canal was finally opened to traffic in 1811.

The Colne Valley, to the west of Huddersfield, is representative of industrial West Yorkshire. Towns with evocative names – Milnsbridge, Linthwaite, Slaithwaite and Marsden – are threaded along the River Colne like beads on a string. In the 18th century this was a landscape of scattered farms and hand-loom weavers, mostly situated on the higher ground. As with Calderdale, a few miles to the north, the deep-cut valley of the Colne was transformed by the Industrial Revolution. Once the textile processes began to be mechanised, mills were built in the valley bottom. They specialised in the production of fine worsted cloth. The River Colne provided the power for the first mills, and the canal subsequently improved the transport links.

The mills grew larger as water power gave way to steam, towering over the rows of terraced houses built in their shadows. Throughout this walk you can see the mill chimneys and the sawtooth roof-lines of the weaving sheds, though some mills are in ruins and others are now given over to other trades. Slaithwaite (often pronounced 'Slowitt') is typical of the textile towns in the Colne Valley. It looks to be an unlikely spa town, but that's what it became in the 1820s, albeit briefly, when its mineral springs were compared favourably with those of Harrogate. Now, with the canal restored, Slaithwaite is finding another new lease of life and you'll find a range of independent shops and cafés when you visit.

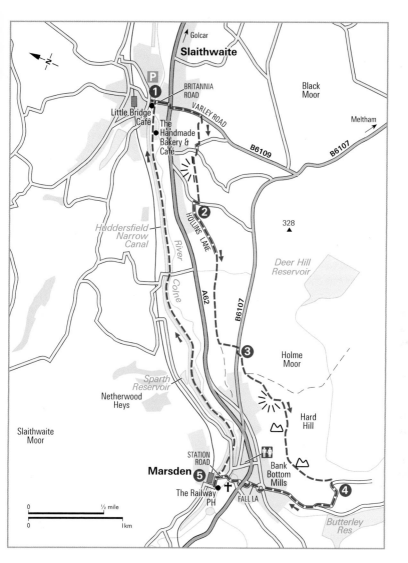

1. Begin along Britannia Road, turning right on to the A62 and crossing to continue up Varley Road. Beyond the last house, go through a squeeze gap on the right and climb to a field. Swinging right and left, follow an indistinct path to a stile on the opposite side. Carry on beside the right-hand wall, crossing through a gate to a tarmac lane. Follow it right and left to a crossroads. Take the track opposite, bearing left after 20yds (18m) on to another track between houses. Go over a stile at the end, keep ahead at the edge of successive fields, crossing more stiles and eventually leaving beside a house on to a tarmac lane.

2. Go briefly right before turning left along a track that ultimately leads to a farm. Walk forwards past the front of a cottage (through the garden), passing through a dilapidated gate into a field corner. Carry on ahead, negotiating

15

gates either side of a beck at the far side and passing an abandoned farmstead to a walled path. Where the path shortly veers right, take the gate ahead into a field. Follow the right wall, bearing slightly left beyond its end to slant up across rough pastures. Go over a stile and keep forwards, continuing on to reach a walled path. Climb left to another stile, then turn right down to a bend. Scaling a wall stile on the left, walk away at the bottom edge of fields to a kissing gate. Continue through a plantation, swinging left at the far side along a path up to the B6107.

3. Walk right for 75yds (69m), then take a track off to the left. Continue past a house and through a gate, shortly reaching a fork. Keep ahead on the right branch. Cross a beck and fork left uphill; the way narrows to a path. At a junction turn right to pass below old quarries on the shoulder of Hard Hill. Climb to a kissing gate, then drop to a bridge beside a stone aqueduct. After rising to a memorial bench, the way levels and Butterley Reservoir comes into view. Beyond another kissing gate by a small stone building, climb left to a stile, carrying on over a second stile and out on to a metalled track. Follow it down to a tarmac lane.

4. Continue downhill, eventually passing terraced houses dwarfed by Bank Bottom Mills. Keep straight ahead at a roundabout along Fall Lane, bearing left before the end to pass beneath the main road. Keep left over a bridge and then right past the church. At the end go left up Station Road.

5. Join the Huddersfield Narrow Canal towpath opposite The Railway pub. Follow it right, dropping past the first of many locks, for a pleasant 3-mile (4.8km) walk back to Slaithwaite.

Where to eat and drink

The Railway, close to the rail station and canal in Marsden, comes at the halfway point of the walk. Slaithwaite itself has a great selection of cafés and pubs. The Handmade Bakery and Café and the Little Bridge Café Wine Bar are both on the canal towpath.

What to see

Sparth Reservoir, located next to the towpath between Marsden and Slaithwaite, is used to top up water in the canal. It has been a local wild swimming spot since the 1950s and has seen community swimming events held there in the past. Near Slaithwaite is the country's only working guillotine gate on a narrow canal.

While you're there

Slaithwaite has a number of independent art and craft and antique shops selling work from local artists. The Colne Valley Museum in Golcar (open Saturday, Sunday and Bank Holiday Mondays, noon till 4pm) is based in an old weaver's cottage and has information about the local area. You can either drive there or reach it by walking a further 1.5 miles (2.4km) along the canal towpath.

STANDEDGE FROM MARSDEN

DISTANCE/TIME	8.25 miles (13.3km) / 4hrs
ASCENT/GRADIENT	1,215ft (370m) / ▲ ▲
PATHS	Old tracks and byways, canal towpath, several stiles
LANDSCAPE	Heather moorland
SUGGESTED MAP	OS Explorer OL21 South Pennines
START/FINISH	Grid reference: SE047118
DOG FRIENDLINESS	Keep under control where sheep graze on open moorland
PARKING	Standedge Tunnel car park by Marsden Station
PUBLIC TOILETS	Peel Street in Marsden town centre

Trans-Pennine travel has, until quite recently, been a hazardous business. Over the centuries many routes have been driven across the hills to link the industrial centres of West Yorkshire and Lancashire. Some paths were consolidated into paved causeways for packhorse traffic, before being upgraded to take vehicles. This track, linking the Colne Valley to Rochdale and Milnrow in Lancashire, was known as the Rapes Highway.

The Standedge Tunnel

This was tough terrain for building a canal. When the Huddersfield Narrow Canal was cut, to provide a link between Huddersfield and Ashton-under-Lyne, there was one major obstacle for the canal builders to overcome: the gritstone bulk of Standedge. There was no way round; the canal had to go through. The Standedge Tunnel, extending 3 miles (4.8km) from Marsden to Diggle, was a monumental feat of engineering. Costly in every sense, it took 17 years to build and many navvies lost their lives. The result was the longest, highest and deepest canal tunnel in the country. In an attempt to keep those costs down, the tunnel was cut as narrow as possible, which left no room for a towpath. Towing horses had to be led over the hills to the far end of the tunnel, near Diggle in Lancashire. The bargees had to negotiate Standedge Tunnel using their own muscle power alone. This method, known as 'legging', required them to lie on their backs and push with their feet against the sides and roof of the tunnel. This operation would typically take a back-breaking four hours. Closed to canal traffic for many years, the tunnel was reopened in 2001. It is now a major tourist attraction and includes boat trips and a visitor centre.

A rebellion in Marsden

In 1812 Marsden became the focus for the 'Luddite' rebellion against mechanisation in the textile industry. A secret group of croppers and weavers banded together to break up the new machinery that was appearing in local mills. Eventually the army was despatched to restore order. Some 60 men were put on trial for their part in the troubles; 17 of them were hanged.

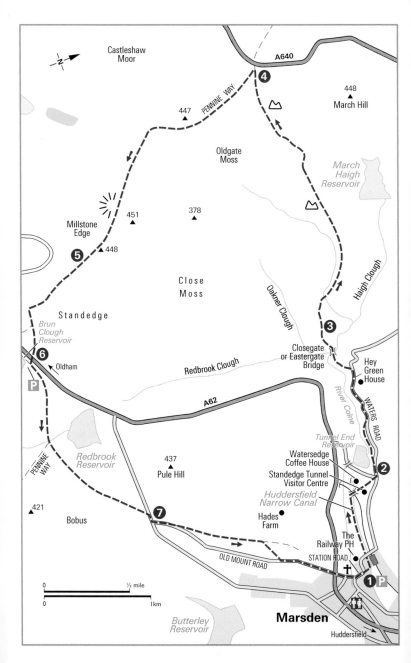

1. From the car park, turn right and then bear right, following the Huddersfield Narrow Canal towpath away from a lock. Approaching Tunnel End, where both canal and railway disappear into tunnels, leave the towpath to cross a footbridge. Bear right uphill past the visitor exhibition to a T-junction with a house (the old Tunnel End Inn) directly in front.

2. Turn left on to Waters Road. Almost immediately, leave through a gate on the left for a path paralleling the road. After rejoining, keep straight ahead past the entrance to Hey Green House. About 100yds (91m) further on, bear left, just before a cottage, on to a bridleway. The path takes you across Closegate Bridge, known locally as Eastergate Bridge, where two becks meet.

3. Swing right, following the beck for about 100yds (91m), before forking left at a waymarker into a narrow side valley. The path levels higher up, curving towards the rounded prominence of March Hill, now intermittently marked by stone waypoints. After a final stiff pull, the path descends towards the A640.

4. Immediately before reaching the road, turn sharp left at a Pennine Way sign over a wooden bridge spanning a little beck. The onward path rises and falls over the moss for just over 0.75 miles (1.2km) to a junction at the abrupt lip of Standedge. Go left along the top of the scarp, enjoying the panoramic view across East Lancashire.

5. Beyond the trig point, the path gently loses height, passing through successive gates and across broken walls to emerge on to a track. Follow it left out to the A62, where a car park overlooks Brun Clough Reservoir.

6. Cross the road and take steps up to the left from the car park. Signed 'Pennine Way', the path parallels the deep road cutting before turning away across Marsden Moor. To the left is Redbrook Reservoir, with Pule Hill beyond. Approaching a marker stone, bear left at a footpath sign, dipping across a stream to continue over the moss. Eventually, after 0.75 miles (1.2km), the way narrows and drops steeply to a stream in a gully. Climb beyond to a road.

7. Turn right and then immediately left on to Old Mount Road. After 50yds (46m), bear left again, along a stony track signed to Hades Farm. After 0.5 miles (800m), watch for a discreet sign just off the track for a path that leads to a small gate and descends beside a wall to rejoin Old Mount Road. Continue downhill, crossing the main road into Towngate. Bear left past the church and at the end go left again up Station Road back to the car park.

Where to eat and drink
The Watersedge Coffee House (open Thursday to Sunday) by the entrance to the Standedge Tunnel serves light refreshments, or for more standard pub fare try The Railway by the start of the walk in Marsden, where walkers are very welcome and food is served daily.

What to see
In spring and early summer, listen out for the cuckoo. If an old story is to be believed, the people of Marsden realised that when the cuckoo arrived, so did the sunshine. They tried to keep spring forever, by building a tower around the cuckoo. As the last stones were about to be laid, however, the cuckoo flew away. The people of Marsden celebrate Cuckoo Day in April each year.

While you're there
The Standedge Tunnel Visitor Centre has fascinating films and collections telling the story of the tunnel and people – from its planning and through over 200 years of history.

HOLMFIRTH AND THE HOLME VALLEY

DISTANCE/TIME	4.5 miles (7.2km) / 2hrs 30min
ASCENT/GRADIENT	800ft (244m) / ▲
PATHS	Good paths and tracks, several stiles
LANDSCAPE	Upland pasture
SUGGESTED MAP	OS Explorer 288 Bradford & Huddersfield
START/FINISH	Grid reference: SE143084
DOG FRIENDLINESS	On lead in fields with livestock, off on lanes
PARKING	Crown Bottom car park on Market Street or Sands Lane long stay car park
PUBLIC TOILETS	At Sands Lane long stay car park

Holmfirth and the Holme Valley have been popularised as 'Summer Wine Country', forever linked to the whimsical TV series *Last of the Summer Wine*, written by Roy Clarke and starring a trio of incorrigible old buffers, Compo, Foggy and Clegg. The cast were familiar faces in the town until the series ended in 2010 after running for 37 years. When Londoner Bill Owen (lovable rogue Compo) died in 1999 at the age of 85, he was laid to rest overlooking the little town he had grown to call home. Visitors come to Holmfirth in their droves, in search of film locations such as Sid's Café and Nora Batty's house. But Holmfirth takes its TV fame in its stride, for this isn't the first time that the town has starred in front of the cameras. In fact, Holmfirth very nearly became another Hollywood. Bamforths, better known for its naughty seaside postcards, began to make short films here in the early years of the last century. They were exported around the world to popular demand. Local people were drafted in as extras in Bamforths' overwrought dramas. Film production came to an end at the outbreak of World War I and, sadly, was never resumed.

Holmfirth town, much more than just a film set, is the real star along with the fine South Pennine scenery that surrounds it. By the time you have completed half of this walk, you are a mile (1.6km) from the Peak National Park. The town grew rapidly with the textile trades, creating a tight-knit community in the valley bottom: a maze of ginnels, alleyways and narrow lanes. The River Holme, which runs through its middle, has flooded on many occasions. but the most devastating flood occurred back in 1852, when, after heavy rain, Bilberry Reservoir burst its banks. The resulting torrent of water destroyed the centre of Holmfirth and claimed 81 lives.

In more recent times, Holmfirth has become something of a hub for road cyclists. The Tour de France Grand Depart passed through here in 2014 on its way up the infamous Holme Moss. Subsequent Tour de Yorkshire routes (a legacy of the Grand Depart) have passed through the town, drawing huge crowds to cheer on the cyclists.

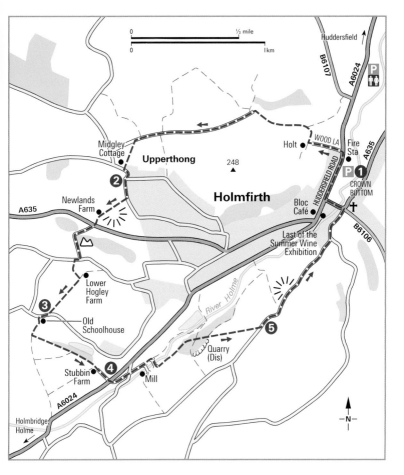

1. From Crown Bottom car park, walk to the right along Huddersfield Road for just 100yds (91m) before bearing left just after the fire station, up Wood Lane. The road soon narrows to a steep track. Keep left of a house and through a gate, to continue on a walled path. At the top of the hill, by a bench, follow the road to the right, leading to a track. Follow this track, soon enclosed, as it wheels left, down into a valley. Soon after you approach woodland, you have a choice of tracks: keep left on the walled path, uphill. When it eventually joins a stone farm track, turn left and after about 50yds (46m), climb steps on the left to cross a stile. Immediately afterwards, go through a swing gate and across a field path to another gate. Walk on an enclosed path to a track. Turn left to join another enclosed path before emerging on a road by Midgley Cottage. Turn left and follow the road as it bends through the top of the village.

2. Continue along the road, which wheels round to the right. Walk downhill, with great views opening up of the Holme Valley. After 150yds (137m) on the road, take a cinder track on the right. Walk down to meet a road. Cross over and take the tarmac lane ahead, steeply down into a little valley and up the other side. When this minor road forks at the top, go right, uphill. Immediately

after the first house, go left on a gravel track. Follow this track to Lower Hogley Farm, where you keep right, past a knot of houses, to a gate and stile. Cross this on to a field path, with a wall to your left. Go through four fields, aiming for the mast on the horizon, and descend to the road.

3. Go right for just 50yds (46m) to bear left around a path. Follow the walled footpath downhill, through a gate; as the footpath opens out into a grassy area, bear left on a grass track down into the valley. Go over a stile next to a gate, following an enclosed path above woodland. On approaching houses, cross a stile and join a metalled track at a fork. Bear right here, then immediately left, on a narrow footpath between houses. Follow a field path, keeping right at a fork to go through a gate; pass houses and continue downhill past Stubbin Farm to meet the main A6024 road.

4. Cross the road, then, by a row of diminutive cottages, take Old Road to the left. Keep straight ahead when you reach a junction between houses, down Water Street. Beyond a mill, cross the River Holme on a metal footbridge and follow a riverside path. The path opens into a field; approximately 20yds (18m) later, fork right over duckboards. Keep to the right (uphill) and cross a stile to enter woodland. Continue in the same direction, following the uphill fork to the right until you reach some steps to the right. Go down the steps and turn right and immediately left, continuing in the same direction (uphill) to emerge at a field. Cross two fields and join a track by a house. Pass some more cottages to meet a road.

5. Go left, along the road. Enjoy fine views down into the Holme Valley as you descend to a junction. Turn left and continue on the long downhill road into Holmfirth.

Where to eat and drink
With so many visitors, Holmfirth is well supplied with pubs and tea shops, where you can stop for refreshments. Bloc Café serves a brunch-style menu of toasty treats and is located opposite the gallery of famous Yorkshire artist Ashley Jackson.

What to see
Holmfirth seems to have grown without much help from town planners. It is an intriguing maze of ginnels, stone steps and small cobbled alleyways, rising up between gritstone houses. After a few minutes' climb you will be rewarded with a view over the roofscape of the town. A *Last of the Summer Wine* exhibition is located on Scarfold, near the River Holme.

While you're there
If you drive through Holmfirth on the A6024, you pass Holmbridge, then Holme, before the Holme Valley comes to a dramatic end, surrounded by a huge sweep of rugged moorland and splendid views. As you climb steeply to the height of Holme Moss, topped with a television mast, you enter the Peak National Park. The area also boasts a vineyard, situated on the hills above Holmbridge.

DOVESTONE AND CHEW RESERVOIRS

DISTANCE/TIME	7 miles (11.3km) / 4hrs 30min
ASCENT/GRADIENT	1,400ft (427m) / ▲ ▲ ▲
PATHS	Generally hard and rocky, some boggy patches on moorland top, some stiles
LANDSCAPE	Steep hillsides with rocky outcrops and open moorland
SUGGESTED MAP	OS Explorer OL1 Peak District – Dark Peak Area
START/FINISH	Grid reference: SE013034
DOG FRIENDLINESS	Mostly open sheep country subject to access agreements; dogs should be kept on lead or under close control at all times
PARKING	Car park below Dovestone Reservoir dam (daily charge)
PUBLIC TOILETS	By car park

Around 130 years ago, as the demands of Manchester's industrial population grew, the need to supply the city with safe and sufficient drinking water became paramount. Inevitably the planners turned their attentions towards the Pennines, that formidable upland barrier that soaks up so much of northern England's rain. Before long a series of reservoirs sprang up across the hills that separated urban Lancashire and Yorkshire and, just as the counties' rivers and streams had previously been harnessed for the mills, now the moorlands were drained and the tiny Pennine valleys dammed to create artificial lakes. The first of the four reservoirs collectively known as Dovestones was Yeoman Hey, constructed in 1880, and followed by Greenfield in 1902. When Chew Reservoir was built, 10 years later, it was the highest in Britain at around 1,600ft (488m). Dovestone Reservoir is the largest of the group and was completed in 1967. When Yeoman Hey was being planned, local mill owners were concerned that it would deprive them of essential water, so a tunnel was constructed from the confluence of Birchen Clough and Holme Clough to the Ashway Gap. This ensured water would continue flowing into Greenfield Brook, down a stepped weir, for use in the mills.

Today the four vital reservoirs supply drinking water to Oldham and communities in the Tame Valley. They are owned and run by United Utilities, which provides water to nearly 3 million homes in northwest England. United Utilities actively encourages certain types of recreation around its reservoirs. Swimming is forbidden, because of the deep water and outlet pipes that can cause dangerous undercurrents, but sailing and windsurfing are enjoyed on Dovestone Reservoir, with regular races taking place. On the adjoining hillside there are two orienteering routes: look out for the small posts with helpful coloured markings and numbers. The popular 2.5-mile (4km) track around the shore of Dovestone Reservoir has been made suitable for wheelchair users, while the numerous paths and bridleways that explore the surrounding moors include the Oldham Way. The course of this superb circular, 40-mile (64.3km) walking route around the borough of Oldham can be seen as you set off from Dovestone Reservoir. It runs high and straight across the hillside to the south, on the route of a former steam tramway that was built a hundred years ago to aid the construction of Chew Reservoir.

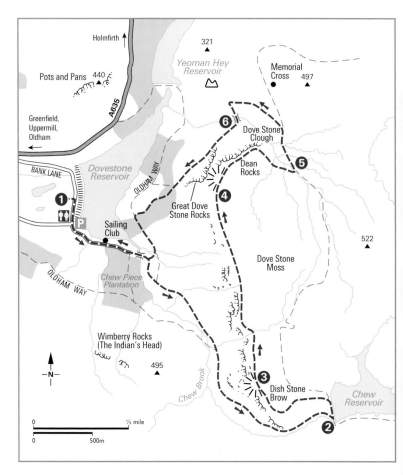

1. From the car park walk up to the top of the Dovestone Reservoir dam and turn right, along the road past the sailing club. Where the plantation ends go over a bridge and keep straight on to follow a private service track that winds its way steadily up to the very top of the Chew Valley.

2. When you reach Chew Reservoir turn left and walk along the top of the dam. Just before it kinks right, drop to the foot of the embankment. Ignore a footpath sign over to the right and, with your back to the dam, head away along a broad but indistinct peaty path. Before long, the way becomes clearer and gradually firmer underfoot, curving gently to the right and joining the rocky edge above Dish Stone Brow.

3. With Dovestone Reservoir coming into view far below, continue along the high rim of the hillside past a series of rocky outcrops. After almost a mile (1.6km), the way passes the ruin of Bramley's Cottage, built into the lee of a great boulder, and continues to a prominent cairn on Fox Stone above Great Dove Stone Rocks.

4. Beyond Great Dove Stone Rocks, the edge swings in above the deep, narrowing valley of Dove Stone Clough. After crossing a side stream, the path eventually reaches the head of the clough.

5. Cross another stream as it flows over a rocky shelf and head back above the opposite side of the ravine. Watch for a fork (grid ref SE 031040) and bear left, contouring the hill and dropping gently towards the reservoir. Keep left again as it splits once more a little further on (grid ref SE 031042). The monument seen ahead and above is a memorial to James Platt, who was killed nearby in a shooting accident in 1857. Now descending more purposefully, the path leads to a fence stile with a dog gate. Cross and turn left on a narrow path, contouring back through bracken towards the mouth of a tunnel bringing water from the valley head above Greenfield Reservoir. Keep left at a fork in the path, then cross another path, keeping straight ahead through bracken on a narrow path in the direction of the tunnel (in summer, when the bracken is high, it may be difficult to see the start of this path). Drop steeply to a stile and cross the aqueduct on a high footbridge.

6. Climb away to a stile and continue beside a fence through rocky debris beneath the impressive towering cliffs of Dean Rocks and Great Dove Stone Rocks. Eventually the path falls gently along a wide, grassy strip between a maturing plantation of conifers. Go through a gate and drop down across a rough, open pasture to reach the popular reservoir-side track. Turn left and follow this track all the way back to the car park.

Where to eat and drink
On sunny weekends there may be an ice-cream van in the Dovestones car park. Otherwise, the nearest place for refreshments is a pub called The Clarence, about a mile (1.6km) away in Greenfield.

What to see
When walking from Dovestones to Chew Reservoir, look up high to Wimberry Rocks on your right. By tilting your head slightly to the right, you should be able to make out the famous Indian's Head. Later, as you stand on the edge of the moors above Dovestone Reservoir, a small but distinctively pointed hill a mile (1.6km) beyond the reservoir (and topped by a war memorial) tends to catch the eye. It's known as Pots and Pans and its odd-shaped rocks contain weathered holes that were once rumoured to have held the wine of well-to-do grouse shooters.

While you're there
A visit to the Saddleworth Museum and Art Gallery, which is located just 2.5 miles (4km) from Dovestones on the High Street in Uppermill, is highly recommended. The former canalside woollen mill is full of curiosities and includes hands-on exhibits for children and informative displays.

LONGDENDALE AND THE WILD PENNINES

DISTANCE/TIME	7.5 miles (12km) / 4hrs
ASCENT/GRADIENT	1,560ft (475m) / ▲ ▲
PATHS	Good paths and tracks, moorland path may be boggy in wet weather, some stiles
LANDSCAPE	Heather moorland and rolling farm pastures
SUGGESTED MAP	OS Explorer OL1 Peak District – Dark Peak Area
START/FINISH	Grid reference: SK072992
DOG FRIENDLINESS	Walk is on farmland and access agreement land; dogs should be kept on lead
PARKING	Crowden car park
PUBLIC TOILETS	At Crowden and Torside car park

Longdendale, the valley of the River Etherow, threads deep into the Pennines between the craggy cliffs of Bleaklow and the sullen slopes of Black Hill. In bygone centuries this must have been an inhospitable but dramatic wilderness of heath and bog. Meanwhile, in nearby Manchester, the Industrial Revolution had caused a dramatic increase in the population from around 10,000 to over 230,000. This meant that Manchester needed more water, and its engineers turned to Longdendale. Between 1848 and 1877 a string of five reservoirs were built to the designs of John Frederick La Trobe Bateman. Later came the railway, linking Manchester with Sheffield, then came electricity. So this remote narrow valley was filled with the contraptions of the modern world. Manchester's people came here in their thousands, using the railway and taking to the hills.

Pennine wayfarers

Crowden, where the walk starts, is one of the few settlements in the valley. Around the campsite you'll often see weary walkers with heavy backpacks. More often than not they will have just completed the first day of the Pennine Way over Kinder Scout and Bleaklow. In the book they're clutching, Alfred Wainwright has told them how unsightly Longdendale is, and how they will continue towards the horrors of Black Hill's bogs. But this walk shows you the very best of Longdendale. The railway has gone now, dismantled in 1981 with the decline of the coal industry. After strolling down to the Torside Reservoir you follow its trackbed, now part of the Longdendale Trail. Soon you've left the valley behind and you're climbing through the shade of woods. Longdendale looks pretty good now. Bleaklow's ruffled peat-hagged top is fronted by a bold line of cliffs, which overlook the valley's lakes and fields. Several streams plummet down shady ravines, while Torside Clough, a huge gash in the side of the fell, dwarfs the little farm at its foot. Now you're on the moors with the squat cliffs of Millstone Rocks lying across cottongrass moors. At Lad's Leap, the Hollins Clough stream tumbles over a slabbed rocky bed into Coombes

Clough. Despite the name, you should descend to ford the stream before continuing above Highstone Rocks to the rim of the Crowden Valley, where you can look deep into the inner recesses of Black Hill. Below, your car awaits.

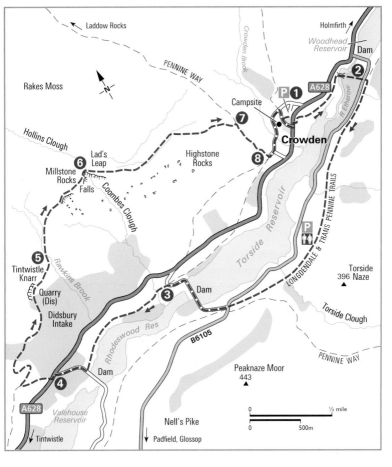

1. Leave the car park via the path from the toilet block, cross the main road, turn left and then go right at a kissing gate. Turn though a second gate (signed 'Woodhead Dam') a short way along on the left. Walk past Torside Reservoir to cross the River Etherow below the Woodhead Dam. Climb away to the road.

2. Cross to a path opposite, which leads up to the Longdendale and Trans Pennine trails. Follow the trackbed right for 1.75 miles (2.8km) to meet the road again. Cross and go right, then left on a wide descending track (Pennine Way) that swings across the valley over the Torside Dam. Stay on the tarmac road as it climbs away left. Leave the road when it bends right, walking ahead to the left of two gates

3. Go through the gate and follow the path through some scrub woodland to reach the Rhodeswood Dam, where a tarmac lane takes you back to the main road.

4. Diagonally opposite, a gated track rises on to the moor. Swing right at a bend, then bear left at a fork, soon climbing around another bend. Ignore a sharp right and turn though a final bend, now heading for the top of a plantation. Go over a stile there, and climb on, shortly passing below the cliffs of a quarry.

5. The path then narrows and soon turns up to a stile beside Rawkins Brook. Go over the stile and bear right, away from the fence line, across the stream to follow a peaty path northeast towards the high ground of Millstone Rocks.

6. On reaching the edge, follow it right to Lad's Leap, turning in to ford the stream. Now diverging from the edge, a clear path runs on, soon crossing a broken wall to descend along a shallow trough. Joining another wall for a while, the descent gradually steepens and eventually drops off the nose of the hill to a small copse.

7. Now on the Pennine Way, go through a gate on the right and follow the ongoing path across successive fields to reach a track.

8. To the left, the track falls across the foot of Crowden Brook and continues to a farm. Walk on past large sheds, then, through a gate, turn right beside a campsite. At a toilet block, fork left back to the car park.

Where to eat and drink

Hot and cold drinks, ice creams and confectionery are available from the campsite shop at Crowden (open to the public in season). For pub meals, visit the Peels Arms on Temple Street, Padfield (off Glossop Road). It is a traditional village pub, serving decent ale and good food daily.

What to see

The Longdendale Trail was the trackbed for the Great Central Railway's Woodhead line, built in 1845 to link Manchester and Sheffield. The line, which included the 3-mile (4.8km) Woodhead Tunnel through the Pennine ridge, claimed many lives – 32 for the tunnel alone. Those who died in the hostile damp conditions are unrecorded, but 28 workers perished in a cholera epidemic of 1849 while building a second Woodhead Tunnel. Some of the graves can be seen at Woodhead Chapel, just off the route above the Woodhead Reservoir's dam.

While you're there

It's worth doing a short there-and-back walk along the Pennine Way to see Laddow Rocks. The fine tiered gritstone cliffs, which lie in the heart of the Crowden Valley, were popular with climbers in the early 1900s. Today, most of the climbers have moved on to the more challenging (and accessible) eastern edges, such as Stanage, Curbar and Froggat.

BLEAKLOW'S PEATLANDS

DISTANCE/TIME	7.75 miles (12.5km) / 5hrs
ASCENT/GRADIENT	1,700ft (518m) / ▲ ▲
PATHS	Unsurfaced tracks and sometimes indistinct moorland paths (good navigation skills advised), several stiles
LANDSCAPE	High peat moor
SUGGESTED MAP	OS Explorer OL1 Peak District - Dark Peak Area
START/FINISH	Grid reference: SK039943
DOG FRIENDLINESS	Walk is on access agreement land; dogs should be kept on lead
PARKING	Manor Park car park, off Glossop High Street East (A57)
PUBLIC TOILETS	By Manor Park café
NOTES	The route is unsuitable for inexperienced walkers in poor visibility

Bleaklow's not so much a hill, more a vast expanse of bare black peat, where even the toughest moor grasses can't take root. Wainwright once wrote that nobody loved the place, and those who got on it were glad to get off. But there's another side to Bleaklow. There are corners where bilberries grow thick round fascinating rock sculptures; where heather, bracken and grass weave a colourful quilt. Places like Grinah Stones, Yellowslacks and Shepherd's Meeting Stones are all remote, but they're dramatic places, far superior to anything seen on the popular routes. Bleaklow's true top lies in the midst of the mires, but only a few feet lower is Higher Shelf Stones, a bold summit with a distinctive mountain shape and some good crags. Climb Higher Shelf Stones from Old Glossop, and you'll see the best of Bleaklow.

Time has been kind to Old Glossop. Planners and industrialists of the 19th and 20th centuries built their shops and factories further west, leaving the old quarter untouched. Here 17th-century cottages of darkened gritstone line cobbled streets, overlooked by the spired All Saints Church. Shepley Street takes you into the hills, and it's not long before you're climbing the heathery spur of Lightside and looking across the rocky ravine of Yellowslacks. A fine path develops on the cliff edge before entering the confines of Dowstone Clough, which clambers towards Higher Shelf Stones. Eventually the clough shallows and the stream becomes a trickle in the peat, leaving you to find your own way. Sandy channels, known as groughs, lead you southwards.

From the summit rocks you look down on the deep twisting clough of Shelf Brook and out across the plains of Manchester to the shadowy hills of north Wales. Leaving the high moors is a faint path across a grassy spur descending into Shelf Brook's clough, where you join the Doctor's Gate track. This gets its name from Doctor Talbot, the Vicar of Glossop, who paved the packhorse route over the moors to make hist visits to his father in Sheffield easier. His trips were worthy of note because he was in fact the illegitimate son of the very powerful Earl of Shrewsbury. Much earlier, the old highway was used by Roman troops marching between their forts at Navio (Brough, near Hope) and Melandra (Glossop).

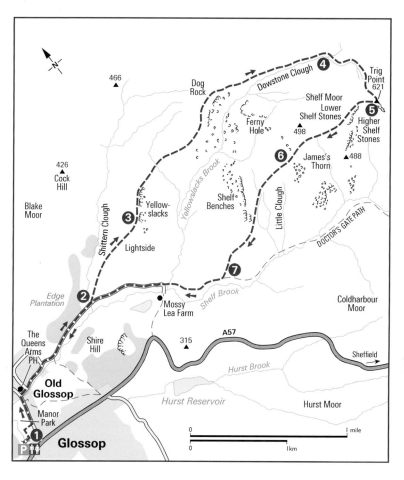

1. From the car park, cross a bridge and walk through Manor Park, passing the café to emerge on to Manor Park Road. Turn left towards Old Glossop and then right along Shepley Street, passing a factory, to a bus turning circle. Continue eastwards on a farm track, between the partially wooded dome of Shire Hill on the right and the wooded slopes of Edge Plantation on the left.

2. On reaching a gate, leave the track through a kissing gate on the left. The path, confined at first by a fence and dry-stone wall, climbs northeast on a pastured spur overlooking the curiously named but pleasant craggy valley of Shittern Clough. In the upper reaches and beyond a second kissing gate, the now well-defined path continues the climb through bilberry bushes and then over the heather of Upper Lightside.

3. The path settles along the spur's southern brow high above Yellowslacks Brook. A dilapidated wire fence comes in from the right and the path goes along the left-hand side of it before joining the cliff edges of Yellowslacks and Dog Rock. The crags close in to form the rugged channel of Dowstone Clough and the path slips through the fence posts. Towards the top, the path joins the stream in the now shallow clough to avoid the peat haggs.

4. Eventually the stream divides among a bed of rushes (grid ref SK 088953). Cross the main stream and follow the snaking tributary gully, which soon curves east and then south through a complex of peat haggs. The summit of Higher Shelf Stones lies just over 0.25 miles (400m) to the south, but remains hidden until the last moment, when the trig column suddenly appears a short distance to the right, perched atop a rocky slab.

5. From Higher Shelf Stones, leave the trig column in a northerly direction and after approximately 20yds (18m), curve left skirting the edge of the peat haggs to pick up a narrow path towards Lower Shelf Stones. Carry on to the shoulder of James's Thorn, where a grass path forks off left to the second crash site (see 'What to see'). The way back continues beside the peat (with the peat haggs to the right and moorland to the left) over the crest, dropping to a fence stile by a small pool.

6. Now clear, the path descends across the grassy hillside, later settling beside the gully of a stream. Passing through a broken wall, it joins a track from the right and continues as a broader track, eventually meeting Doctor's Gate Path by a stone barn.

7. Continue down the valley to a junction by Mossy Lea Farm. Bear right, soon picking up the outward route at the foot of Lightside to return to Manor Park.

Where to eat and drink

The small café in Manor Park sells ice creams and snacks throughout the summer season. For more substantial fare, visit The Queens Arms on Shepley Street in Old Glossop.

What to see

Some 200yds (183m) northeast of the summit of Higher Shelf Stones look for the remains of a US Air Force Superfortress bomber, which crashed here in 1948 killing its crew. Walkers have reported seeing ghosts near the site. On the way back you can detour to the rock outcrops on James's Thorn, where there's another plane wreck. A small monument and fragments of wreckage mark the place where, on 18 May 1945, a Canadian Lancaster bomber crashed.

While you're there

Glossop is a fascinating, bustling town to visit. It's known locally as Howard's Town in tribute to its 19th-century benefactors. Bernard Edward Howard, the 12th Duke of Norfolk, was one of the founders of the first cotton mills in the area. By 1831 there were 30 in the town. At this time the grand town hall, the Square and the Roman Catholic church were built.

FROM HAYFIELD TO KINDER DOWNFALL

DISTANCE/TIME	8 miles (12.9km) / 4hrs 30min
ASCENT/GRADIENT	1,590ft (485m) / ▲ ▲ ▲
PATHS	Well-defined tracks and paths, several stiles
LANDSCAPE	Heather and peat moorland and farm pastures
SUGGESTED MAP	OS Explorer OL1 Peak District - Dark Peak Area
START/FINISH	Grid reference: SK048869
DOG FRIENDLINESS	Walk is on farmland and access agreement land; dogs should be kept on lead
PARKING	Bowden Bridge pay car park
PUBLIC TOILETS	Across bridge from car park

If you want to climb one of the quieter ways to Kinder Scout, Hayfield to the west is one of the best places to start. It's also a route with a bit of history to it. From the beginning of the 20th century there had been conflict between ramblers and the owners of Kinder's moorland plateau. By 1932 ramblers from the industrial conurbations of Sheffield and Manchester, disgusted by lack of government action to open up the moors to walkers, decided to hold a mass trespass on Kinder Scout. Benny Rothman, a Manchester rambler and a staunch communist, would lead the trespass on Sunday 24 April. The police expected to intercept Benny at Hayfield railway station, but he outwitted them by arriving on his bicycle, not in the village itself, but at Bowden Bridge Quarry to the east. Here he was greeted by hundreds of cheering fellow ramblers. With the police in hot pursuit, the group made their way towards Kinder Scout. Although they were threatened and barracked by a large gathering of armed gamekeepers, the ramblers still managed to get far enough to join their fellow trespassers from Sheffield, who had come up from the Snake Inn. Predictably, fighting broke out and Benny Rothman was one of five arrested. He was given a four-month jail sentence for unlawful assembly and breach of the peace. The ramblers' cause inspired folk singer Ewan MacColl (famous for 'Dirty Old Town' and 'The First Time Ever I Saw Your Face') to write 'The Manchester Rambler', which became something of an anthem for the proliferating walkers' clubs and societies. However, it took until 1951, when the recently formed National Park negotiated access agreements with the landowners, for the situation to improve. Just like the mass trespass, this walk starts at Bowden Bridge, where you will see a commemorative plaque on the rock face above the car park.

The Downfall

A dark, shadow-filled cleft in the rocks captures your attention. It's the Kinder Downfall, where the infant Kinder tumbles off the plateau. Now you climb to the edge for the most spectacular part of the walk – the part that would have been a trespass all those years ago –and continue along a promenade of dusky gritstone rock. Round the next corner you come to that dark cleft seen earlier. In the dry summer months the fall is a mere trickle, just enough to wet the rocks, but after the winter rains it can turn into a 100ft (30m) torrent. The prevailing west wind often catches the deluge, funnelling it back up to the top rocks like plumes of white smoke. In contrast, the way down is gentle, leaving the edge at Red Brook and descending the pastures of Tunstead Clough Farm. A quiet leafy lane takes you back into the Kinder Valley.

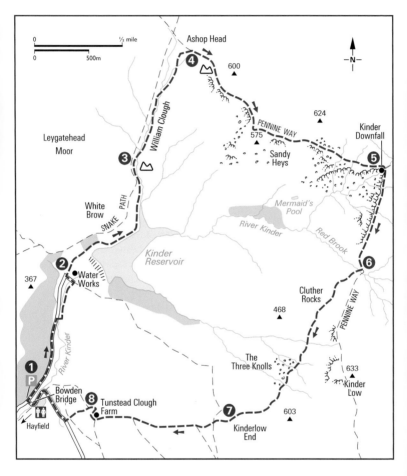

1. Turn left out of the car park and walk up the lane, which winds beneath trees by the River Kinder. After half a mile (800m), cross a bridge and leave the lane along a signposted footpath. It traces the river's east bank before swinging left to rejoin the road at the entrance to a water treatment works.

2. Turn right and go through a pedestrian gate on to a cobbled bridleway that climbs above the buildings. Through a gap, keep ahead above the dam, the path shortly descending to continue beside the reservoir's north shore. Beyond a gate, ignore a footbridge; instead, carry on ahead along a path rising into William Clough, where it is joined by the Snake Path from the left.

3. The path crosses and recrosses the stream as it works its way up the grass and heather clough. Higher up, where the valley divides, keep with the right branch, climbing steps out of the head of the valley to a fork near Ashop Head. Bear right, shortly meeting the Pennine Way at the foot of a steep pull.

4. The climb to gain the summit plateau is soon accomplished and it's easy walking along the edge.

5. Curving in above the rocky combe of the River Kinder, the Kinder Downfall comes into view. Descend to ford the Kinder's shallow rocky channel about 100yds (91m) back from the edge before turning right. Continue along the edge, from where the Mermaid's Pool can be seen.

6. Immediately after crossing Red Brook, bear right at a fork and walk a short distance to a second fork. Keep left, the path briefly rising before settling into a long, gradual descent across the boulder-strewn grass slopes below the edge. The way later passes above the Three Knolls and ultimately descends to a fence gate at the foot of Kinderlow End.

7. Walk on and fork right to a second gate. Continue through a wall gap to follow an indistinct path across successive pastures down a grassy spur. Eventually leaving the hill over a stile, a short grass track leads to Tunstead Clough Farm.

8. Curve around the buildings on a descending gravel track. Lower down, it swings left over a brook and then drops to meet a lane beside a bridge in the upper Sett Valley. Follow the lane straight ahead for about a quarter of a mile (400m) back to Bowden Bridge and the car park.

Where to eat and drink

Near the car park on Kinder Road, The Sportsman Inn is a walker-friendly pub which serves hot and cold food every lunchtime and evening, from snacks to main meals. Children and dogs are welcome and there's a pleasant outside seating area.

What to see

When you're absorbed in the cerebral pleasures of wilderness walking, some comic bird with a flash of red on his head will probably wreck the moment by cackling loudly before scuttling from under your feet. This red grouse will have been absorbed in sampling the tasty heather shoots you're passing. The gamekeeper makes sure that this ungainly bird has all it needs to breed successfully, with a mixture of young heather and mature plants for cover.

While you're there

In 2007, the 75th anniversary of the mass trespass was marked by the opening of the Trespass Trail, a 14-mile (22.5km) walk following the route of the original brave trespassers up on to Kinder Scout.

HAYFIELD AND LANTERN PIKE

DISTANCE/TIME	7.25 miles (11.7km) / 4hrs 30min
ASCENT/GRADIENT	1,345ft (410m) / ▲▲
PATHS	Good paths and tracks, some stiles
LANDSCAPE	Heather moorland and rolling farm pastures
SUGGESTED MAP	OS Explorer OL1 Peak District - Dark Peak Area
START/FINISH	Grid reference: SK035869
DOG FRIENDLINESS	Walk is on farmland and access agreement land; dogs should be kept on lead
PARKING	Sett Valley Trail pay car park, Hayfield
PUBLIC TOILETS	At car park

Hayfield was busy. It had cotton mills, papermaking mills and calico printing and dye factories. Hayfield had times of trouble. Floods washed away three bridges in the town, even swept away some bodies from their churchyard graves. And in 1830 it resounded to the marching feet of a thousand protesting mill workers, demanding a higher wage. As was always the case in such times, the men were beaten back by soldiers and charged with civil disorder. Their industry went into a slow decline that would last a century, and Hayfield returned to its countryside ways.

The Sett Valley Trail and Lantern Pike
The first part of the walk to little Lantern Pike follows the Sett Valley Trail, the trackbed of a railway that until 1970 linked Manchester and New Mills with Hayfield. At its peak the steam train would have brought thousands of people from Manchester. Today it's a pleasant tree-lined track, working its way through the valley between the hills of Lantern Pike and Chinley Churn.

Lantern Pike is the middle of three ridges peeping through the trees, and by the time you get to Birch Vale you're ready to tackle it. You ascend on a shady path through woods, then a country lane with wild flowers, and finally on heather and grass slopes to the rocky-crested summit. Lantern Pike's name comes from the beacon tower that once stood on its summit. It had to be demolished in 1907 after falling into a dangerous state of disrepair. Having descended to the busy Glossop road, the route then climbs up across Middle Moor where it enters a new landscape – one of expansive heather fields. Soon you're on the skyline looking down on the Kinder and the valley. This seems to be complemented to perfection by the shapely and ever-so-green peaks of Mount Famine and South Head.

Into modern Hayfield
You come down to Hayfield on the Snake Path, an old traders' route linking the Sett and Woodland valleys which dates back to 1897. A fine street of stone-built cottages, with window boxes overflowing with flowers, takes you to the centre. It's all so very peaceful...now.

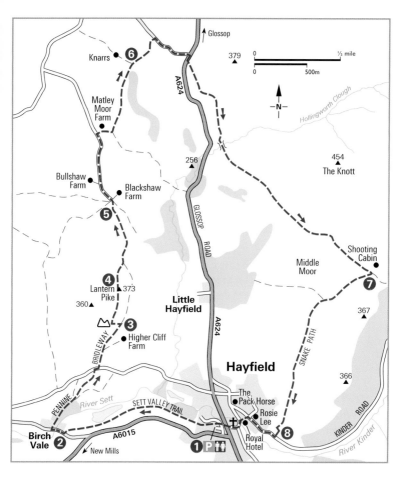

1. Follow the old railway trackbed signed 'The Sett Valley Trail and Pennine Bridleway' from the car park in Hayfield. This heads west down the valley and above the River Sett to meet a minor road close to the A6015 New Mills road at Birch Vale.

2. Turn right along the road, then right again along a rising cobbled track behind the cottages of The Crescent into the shade of the woods. Beyond a gate, the track meets a tarred farm lane at a hairpin bend. Turn left, uphill, to reach a country lane. A surfaced lane, staggered to the right across it, climbs further up the hillside. Keep going past the entrance to Higher Cliff Farm to a gate at the edge of the National Trust's Lantern Pike.

3. Leave the bridleway here and turn left along a grassy wall-lined path, climbing heather and bracken slopes to the rock-fringed ridge. Turn right and climb to Lantern Pike's summit, which is topped by a view indicator.

4. The path continues northwards from the top of Lantern Pike, descending to the northern boundary of the National Trust estate, where it rejoins the track you left earlier. Beyond a gate, keep ahead on the main path which then curves left across a pasture to a five-way footpath signpost near Blackshaw Farm.

5. Go through a gate, turn left along a walled farm lane past Bullshaw Farm, then right at a junction to follow a track in front of Matley Moor Farm. Where the track curves right, leave it and take a rough grassy track on the left. Go over the stile at its end and continue northwards, uphill on a grooved path following the line of the wall. The path ultimately joins a semi-surfaced track from Knarrs.

6. Continue downhill on the track and at the end turn right and walk along the road to reach the A624. Cross this with care and go over the stile at the far side. Turn immediately right, following a faint, rutted track with a wall on the right-hand side. This eventually joins another track before crossing the little valley of Hollingworth Clough on a footbridge before climbing up the heather slopes of Middle Moor.

7. Near a white shooting cabin, turn right on the stony Snake Path. Leave the moor through a gate and curve left to descend across a succession of grazing pastures. A contained track finally leads down to Kinder Road.

8. Turn right to the village. At a fork near the bottom, keep left and immediately left again down a broad passage to come out beside The Royal Hotel. Go right to the street and left past St Matthew's Church, then swing right beside it to the main road. Cross back to the car park.

Where to eat and drink

The Rosie Lee is a traditional tea room on Kinder Road in the centre of Hayfield. The Royal Hotel is spacious, comfortable and welcomes hungry walkers. It has patio seating outside and serves food daily in the bar and restaurant.

What to see

Lantern Pike was donated to the National Trust in 1950, after being purchased by subscription. It stands as a memorial to Edwin Royce, who fought for the freedom to roam these hills. A summit view indicator, commemorating his life, records the 360-degree panorama. When walking back into Hayfield, keep an eye out for the blue commemorative plaque for Arthur Lowe of *Dad's Army* fame, who was born in one of the terraced cottages in 1915.

While you're there

Take a look around Hayfield. It has many old houses, former industrial mills and cottages. The Pack Horse in the centre of the village dates back to 1577. The Royal Hotel was visited by John Wesley in 1755 when it was still the local parsonage.

ALPORT CASTLES AND THE DERWENT VALLEY

DISTANCE/TIME	9.75 miles (15.7km) / 5hrs 30min
ASCENT/GRADIENT	2,200ft (671m) / ▲ ▲
PATHS	Well-defined paths and tracks in forests and on moorland, some stiles
LANDSCAPE	Afforested hillsides and peaty moorland
SUGGESTED MAP	OS Explorer OL1 Peak District - Dark Peak Area
START/FINISH	Grid reference: SK173893
DOG FRIENDLINESS	Much is across farmland and access agreement land; dogs should be kept on lead
PARKING	Fairholmes pay car park
PUBLIC TOILETS	At car park

The walk begins in the Derwent Valley, beneath the great stone ramparts of the impressive Derwent Dam. Your start point, Fairholmes car park, has a history all of its own. At the south end, the crumbling foundations of Fairholmes Farm are an evocative reminder that this was once agricultural land. During the construction of the reservoirs the upper car park was a masons' yard reverberating to the sounds of workmen cutting, shaping and dressing stone for the dams. The stone came from the Longshaw Quarry and was transported here by a specially constructed railway, which linked the LMS sidings in Bamford.

England's largest landslip

You don't stay long in the valley – the route has higher things in mind and climbs through Lockerbrook Coppice. After emerging from the trees, the route follows the top edge of the vast Hagg Side spruce plantation before climbing to Bellhag Tor. Here you get the first view of the landslips that have occurred in the region. However, by climbing northwest along the peaty ridge of Rowlee Pasture, England's largest landslip will be revealed beneath your feet. They call it Alport Castles and, as you stand on the edge of the cliff looking across to the Tower, you can see why. A huge gritstone tor towers above a chaotic jumble of tumbled boulders and the grassy mounds that have been separated from the main ridge. The reason for the instability lies in the shales that are squeezed between the tiers of gritstone here. In wetter times, after the last Ice Age, the river eroded these soft bands, resulting in a 0.5-mile (800m) long landslide that dropped 100ft (30m) below the main cliff.

Secret Lovefeast

Your route takes you on a little path down towards Alport Castles Farm. On the first Sunday of every July they hold the Woodlands Lovefeast service in the barn. These non-conformist religious ceremonies started during the reign of Charles II when Presbyterianism was against the law, and the services had to be held in remote places, far from the eyes of the King's loyal subjects.

Past the farm you follow the valley to its meeting with the Ashop Valley. Here an old Roman road that linked forts at Melandra (at Glossop) and Navio (at Brough, near Hope) takes you across the lower grassy slopes of Kinder Scout, where a jaggers' track is waiting to take you down to the site of a former packhorse bridge at Haggwater then over the hill towards Fairholmes.

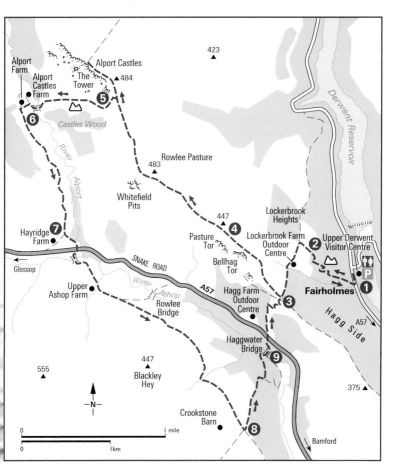

1. The walk begins diagonally opposite the car park exit along a gated track signed 'Lockerbrook'. It climbs through Hagg Side Wood to a bridge over a water leat. Fork left towards Lockerbrook Farm. On meeting a foresters' track, go left, and after 200yds (183m), round a bend, look for a narrow path doubling back left. Climb on, eventually leaving the trees through a gate.

2. Continue up beside a stone wall to come out on to a rough track. Turn left past Lockerbrook Farm.

3. On reaching a junction at the crest by Woodcock Coppice, turn sharp right along a grass path, clambering over a stile towards Bellhag Tor.

4. The path crosses to open moor and becomes paved, tracing the broad spine of Rowlee Pasture. Continue beyond the flags beside a broken wall. The wall

ends just short of the 'Castles' and the way down leaves 100yds (91m) further on, but first wander on above the cliffs to savour the sight.

5. Retrace your steps to the descending path, which drops to follow a boundary. The way remains clear, eventually descending to a footbridge spanning the River Alport.

6. On the far bank, walk 70yds (64m) upstream to a waymarker and climb to a stile. Cross a small field to a track and follow it down the valley from Alport Farm for a mile (1.6km).

7. Where the track curves right, watch for a sign marking a path off left to a stile. Follow this path, passing through trees to the A57. Opposite, a stony track leads to a footbridge over the River Ashop. Follow the track left, shortly joining another from Upper Ashop Farm. At a fork bear right, rising across the shoulder of Blackley Hey to cross Blackley Clough. Carry on for half a mile (800m) to a junction before a gate.

8. Turn left to descend beside a plantation, later passing into the trees. Some 60yds (55m) beyond a sharp right bend, look for an initially indistinct path leaving left and follow it down to Haggwater Bridge.

9. Climb beyond to the A57 and cross to the drive opposite. Where it bends to Hagg Farm Outdoor Centre, keep ahead through a gate on a rising track. Eventually at the top, join a track from the right. Walk on to a junction and go right to reverse your outward route back to Fairholmes.

Where to eat and drink

You can get hot pies, drinks and snacks at the Fairholmes car-park kiosk in spring and summer. The Snake Pass Inn is located a few miles up the Woodlands Valley towards Glossop on the A57 Snake Road. For somewhere closer try the community-owned Anglers Rest pub and café is in the centre of Bamford.

What to see

The leat you can see in Hagg Side Wood is part of a complex system of drains and aqueducts that were built to carry excess water from the Ashop and Alport rivers into the neighbouring Derwent reservoirs. This was a skilfully designed network of flowing water and involved the drilling of a tunnel through the side of the mountain from the Woodlands Valley.

While you're there

Hire a mountain bike from the hire centre in Fairholmes car park. This is an excellent area for cycling and one of the most popular routes is the circuit of the now flooded Derwent Valley. At the head of the valley, at Slippery Stones, is the old packhorse bridge, which was once in the village centre. It was dismantled and rebuilt here when the reservoirs were built. Slippery Stones is also a popular picnic and wild swimming spot.

AROUND BRADFIELD

DISTANCE/TIME	5.75 miles (9.25km) / 3hrs
ASCENT/GRADIENT	500ft (152m) / ▲
PATHS	Minor roads, bridleways and forest paths, few stiles
LANDSCAPE	Woodland, reservoir and meadows
SUGGESTED MAP	OS Explorer OL1 Peak District - Dark Peak Area
START/FINISH	Grid reference: SK262920
DOG FRIENDLINESS	Keep on lead near livestock
PARKING	The Sands car park next to cricket ground
PUBLIC TOILETS	Across the river from car park behind village hall

The Bradfield Scheme

During the Industrial Revolution Sheffield expanded rapidly, as country people sought employment in the city's steel and cutlery works. This put considerable pressure on the water supply. The 'Bradfield Scheme' was Sheffield Waterworks Company's ambitious proposal to build massive reservoirs in the hills around the village of Bradfield, about 8 miles (12.9km) from the city. Work commenced on the first of these, the Dale Dike Dam, on 1 January 1859. It was a giant by the standards of the time with a capacity of over 700 million gallons (3,182 million litres) of water, but some 200 million gallons (910 million litres) less than the present reservoir.

The disaster of 1864

Construction of the dam continued until late February 1864, by which time the reservoir was almost full. Friday 11 March was a stormy day and as one of the dam workers crossed the earthen embankment on his way home, he noticed a crack, about a finger's width, running along it. John Gunson, the chief engineer, turned out with one of the contractors to inspect the dam. They had to make the 8 miles (12.9km) from Sheffield in a horse-drawn gig, in deteriorating weather conditions, so it was 10pm before they got there. After an initial inspection, Gunson concluded that it was probably nothing to worry about. However, as a precaution he decided to lower the water level. He re-inspected the crack at 11.30pm, noting that it had not visibly deteriorated. Then the engineer saw to his horror that water was running over the top of the embankment into the crack. He was making his way to the bottom of the embankment when he felt the ground beneath him begin to shake and saw the top of the dam breached by the straining waters. He just had time to scramble up the side before a large section of the dam collapsed, unleashing a wall of water totalling 650 million gallons (2,955 million litres) down into the valley towards Sheffield. The torrent destroyed everything in its path, and though the waters started to subside within half an hour, their destructive force swept aside 415 houses, 106 factories or shops, 20 bridges and countless cottage and market gardens for 8 miles (12.9km). Few were spared and more than 250 people tragically died. At the inquest the jury concluded that there had been insufficient engineering skill devoted to a work of such size and called for new standards to be met when constructing large-scale structures. The Dale Dike Dam was rebuilt in 1875, but it was not brought into full use until 1887.

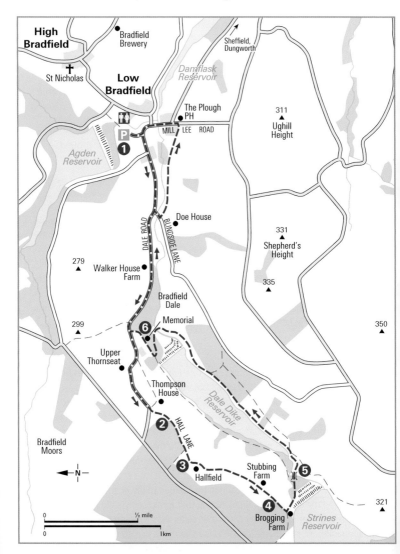

1. Exit the car park and turn right on to the road. At the second junction go right, signed 'Strines and Derwent Valley'. Follow this road uphill, passing, on the right, a former inn, Walker House farm and Upper Thornseat. When the road turns right, with Thompson House below, turn left on to an overgrown track, signposted 'public bridleway'.

2. From here go through a gate in front of you and on to Hall Lane. Follow this along the edge of a wood then through another gate and continue ahead on the farm road. Another gate at the end of this road leads to the entrance to Hallfield.

3. The right of way goes through the grounds of Hallfield, but an alternative permissive path leads left through a gate, round the perimeter of the house and through another gate to rejoin the bridleway at the back of the house. Follow the bridleway through a gate and then past Stubbing Farm.

4. The next gate leads to Brogging Farm and the dam at the head of Strines Reservoir. Look out for a path near the end of the farmhouse and turn left before reaching the dam. Go slightly downhill, through a gate, following the path before crossing through another gate to follow the path in the woods.

5. Cross the stream by a footbridge, go right at a junction immediately afterwards and straight on at the next, keeping left with the stream on your left. Follow the path straight ahead along the bank of Dale Dike Reservoir to the dam head. From here continue through the woods, down several sets of steps, and continue on the path looking out for the memorial on your right, near the road, to those who were killed in 1864.

6. Follow the path until it reaches the road. Cross through a gate and turn right on to the road, proceeding to the road junction. Turn right on to Blindside Lane, cross the bridge then look for a public footpath sign just before the entrance to Doe House. Cross the stile on the left and follow the path all the way to its end on Mill Lee Road, opposite The Plough. Turn left and follow this road downhill, through the village and back to the car park.

Where to eat and drink
The Plough is more than 200 years old and has held a licence for most of that time. A former farmhouse, it contains an enormous stone hearth, stone walls and traditional timbers. Real ales and traditional home-cooked food is the standard fare. Our Cow Molly ice cream parlour is located 6.5 miles (10.5km) away in Dungworth.

What to see
A memorial was erected at the dam in 1991 to commemorate those who lost their lives in the flood. It's a simple memorial stone with an information board. Next to it there's a white stone bearing the letters CLOB. This stands for 'Centre Line of the Old Bank' and marks the site of the original dam wall.

While you're there
Don't miss the Parish Church of St Nicholas in High Bradfield, which dates from the 15th century. Beside the church is the Watch House, which was built in 1745 to prevent bodysnatching and is the last one to survive in Yorkshire. High Bradfield also has its own brewery situated on a working farm and well-known amongst real ale aficionados. The brewery shop is open six days a week.

ASHOPTON AND LADYBOWER

DISTANCE/TIME	5 miles (8km) / 3hrs
ASCENT/GRADIENT	1,074ft (327m) / ▲ ▲
PATHS	Well-defined moorland paths and a reservoir road, no stiles
LANDSCAPE	High gritstone moorland
SUGGESTED MAP	OS Explorer OL1 Peak District - Dark Peak Area
START/FINISH	Grid reference: SK196864
DOG FRIENDLINESS	Keep on lead on access agreement land, can run free by reservoir shores
PARKING	Marked lay-by east of Ashopton Viaduct (A57)
PUBLIC TOILETS	Upper Derwent visitor centre at Fairholmes car park

In the northeast corner of Derbyshire, the heather ridges and gritstone tors of Derwent Edge make one last stand before declining to the plains of Yorkshire. It's always been a sparsely populated corner of the country with few references in the history books. Before World War II, Ashopton, which lay at the confluence of the rivers Derwent and Ashop, was a huddle of stone-built cottages, a small inn and a blacksmith's shop. A little lane ambled from Ashopton northwards to its neighbouring village, Derwent, which enjoyed an even quieter location in the Upper Derwent Valley. But the building of a huge reservoir, the third in the region, shattered the locals' lives. After the completion of its dam in 1943, Ladybower Reservoir gradually filled up, and by 1946 the water level had risen above the rooftops. The forced abandonment of a small north Derbyshire community to quench the thirst of the growing urban masses of the East Midlands may seem harsh today; but paradoxically the flooded, tree-lined valleys of the Upper Derwent are now considered one of the major beauty spots in the Peak District National Park.

Haunting remains

Before you set off, gaze out at the huge concrete viaduct over the reservoir. Wherever you look there is water. Taking a shaded winding track up the next hill, the cottages you see here are all that remain of the village of Ashopton. Soon you're through the woods and heading across open moor to the weathered gritstone tors that top the ridge. The rocks of Whinstone Lee Tor are set into a thick carpet of heather. Though the highest hills in the region lie to the north, this is one of the best viewpoints, as the ridge is at its narrowest here. In the west, Kinder Scout's expansive flat top peeps over Crook Hill's rocky crest.

After passing the Hurkling Stones, the route descends towards the lakeshore in search of Derwent village. The old gateposts of Derwent Hall still survive by the roadside. A notice board shows the position of the hall itself, along with the post office, school, church and some of the old cottages. After a dry spell the water level can sometimes fall sufficiently for you to see the crumbling walls of the village. One small bridge is almost intact, but the villagers dismantled the main twin-arched packhorse bridge for rebuilding beyond the reach of the rising water at Slippery Stones, higher up the valley. Leaving the old village behind you return by the shores of the reservoir. Nature has readjusted. The landscape, though more regimented now, is still beautiful; kestrels still scour the hillside for prey, and dippers frequent the streams as they always have done.

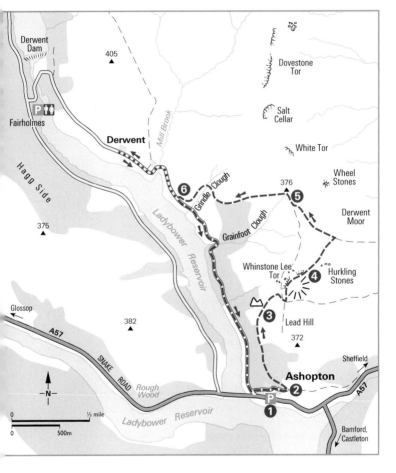

1. Cross the road to a service drive that swings right uphill past Ashopton's remaining cottages before becoming an unsurfaced track.

2. At the top of the track, in a wide turning area, turn sharp left through a small gate. Climb on through trees, keeping left at a fork beside a wall. Passing through a gate, the track emerges from the forest below Lead Hill, where the Ladybower Reservoir comes into view.

3. Soon climbing again through bracken, the path initially remains beside the wall before later turning up towards the corner of a fence and wall. Swing right again up a stony path on to the ridge. At a junction of paths at the top go second left, uphill and along Derwent Edge.

4. The path gently gains height past the boulders of Whinstone Lee Tor and the Hurkling Stones. Broaching a slight crest, the view opens past the Wheel Stones to distant Back Tor. At a cross-path a little further on, go left, signed to Derwent. On reaching a crossing bridleway by a wall, go right and then left through a gate.

5. Carry on downhill to a pine plantation, passing through gates, then ford a stream flowing in Grindle Clough. After winding between a cluster of restored barns, the path, now paved, descends to join the track running along the east bank of Ladybower Reservoir.

6. When the water is low, it's worth a detour (400yds (336m) along the track to the right, at the foot of Mill Brook Clough) to see the fascinating remains of Derwent village. Retrace your steps and continue along the well-graded track, by the shores of the reservoir. After rounding Grainfoot Clough the track passes beneath woodlands with Whinstone Lee Tor crowning the hilltop. The track meets the outward route at a gate above the Ashopton viaduct, opposite the lay-by on the A57 above the reservoir.

Where to eat and drink

The nearest pub is the Yorkshire Bridge on the A6013 at Bamford. Snacks and drinks can also be purchased from the Upper Derwent visitor centre by Derwent Dam.

What to see

The mountain hare is quite common on the moortops. It serves as a reminder of the upland nature of this landscape. In winter its coat changes to a dirty white, to blend with the snow. On clear days, the view before dropping off Derwent Moors is incredible – looking out over the high summits of Win Hill, Lose Hill, Mam Tor, Kinder and Bleaklow.

While you're there

Visit Derwent and Howden Reservoir dams (you can park in Fairholmes car park, south of the Derwent dam). The dams, built between 1912 and 1916, were used in training forays by the Dambusters of 617 Squadron in preparation for their attacks on the Möhne and Eder dams in 1943.

PENNINE WAYS ON KINDER SCOUT

DISTANCE/TIME	9 miles (14.5km) / 5hrs 30min
ASCENT/GRADIENT	1,885ft (575m) / ▲ ▲ ▲
PATHS	Field paths and moorland tracks (mostly slabbed, but some peaty sections)
LANDSCAPE	Rock and peat paths, some steep ascents and descents, occasional scrambly sections
SUGGESTED MAP	OS Explorer OL1 Peak District - Dark Peak Area
START/FINISH	Grid reference: SK123853
DOG FRIENDLINESS	Walk is on farmland and access land; dogs should be kept on lead
PARKING	Edale pay car park
PUBLIC TOILETS	Edale car park and at Moorland centre

In depression-torn 1930s England, Tom Stephenson, then secretary of the Ramblers' Association, told the readers of the *Daily Herald* of his dream to create a long, green trail across the roof of England. This dream would bring Edale to the world's attention. It took 30 years, a mass trespass and Acts of Parliament to achieve, but in 1965 the Pennine Way was opened. Spanning over 250 miles (402km) from Edale to Kirk Yetholm in Scotland, it was Britain's first official long-distance trail. Go to Edale any Friday night and you'll see eager-eyed Pennine Wayfarers making their last-minute preparations.

Popular trail

Unfortunately the popularity of the Way has led to the main route through Grindsbrook being diverted along the foul-weather route up Jacob's Ladder. But as you leave Edale, or to be more strictly correct Grindsbrook Booth (Edale is the name of the valley), you can look across to the old route, which delves deep into the rocky ravine. Your route climbs boldly beside Ringing Roger (the echoing rocks). From this great viewpoint you can look down on the length of Edale and across to the great Lose Hill—Mam Tor ridge. What follows is an edge walk round the great chasm of Grindsbrook, taking you past Nether Tor to the place where the old Pennine Way track comes to meet you. The Way didn't bother with the comforts of the edge, but got stuck into those peat haggs to the right. It was a stiff navigational challenge to get to the Kinder Downfall on the other side of the expansive plateau. Past natural gritstone sculptures and the rocky peak of Grindslow Knoll you come to another ravine, Crowden Brook. The route continues through a fascinating collection of weather-smoothed rocks known as the Wool Packs and on to reach Edale Cross. This rugged gritstone cross marks the highest point on the old packhorse trail between Edale and the Sett Valley. The descent follows the route trod by the hardy mules down Jacob's Ladder, now the new section of the Pennine Way, which you follow via Upper Booth all the way back across the fields to Edale.

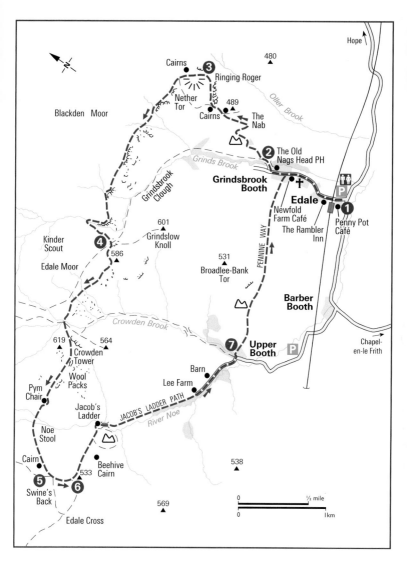

1. Exit the car park beside the public toilets and turn right on to the village road. Go under the railway bridge and through Edale, past The Old Nags Head pub. Eventually fork right at the gate to 'The Gathering' then across a footbridge over Grinds Brook.

2. Leave the main Grindsbrook Clough path by the side of a small barn, forking right to climb up the lower hillside to a gate on the edge of open country. Follow the path, which now zigzags above the valley then climbs above The Nab. Stick with the pitched path until it fades just below the rocks of Ringing Roger then fork right on to a faint rocky path to head more directly on to the ridgeline and summit of Ringing Roger.

3. Follow a few stone flags along the ridgeline leading out to the main path towards Oller Brook. As this veers right, fork left on to a faint path to a group of cairns just right of a lone tree on the edge. Pass two cairns, then fork left on a sandy track before the third. A flagstone lined path now rounds the cavernous hollow of Grindsbrook past Nether Tor. Keep the edge on your left now; you'll cross some small fords before a long indentation to the large ford across the eastern headwater stream of Grinds Brook.

4. Meet the old Pennine Way route at a large cairn by another headwater stream. Ignore a path forking left for the outlier of Grindslow Knoll; instead follow the paved footpath westwards to the head of Crowden Clough (another deep hollow). Continue along the edge of Kinder past the top of Crowden Tower and carry on via a succession of gritstone outcrops: the Wool Packs, Pym Chair and Noe Stool.

5. Continue ahead on the paved path at a large cairn (where the path comes in from Kinder Low). This heads under the Swine's Back – a short angular ridge. Follow the main route left down steps then fork left on slabs at a junction with a sandy path.

6. Continue down to a beehive-shaped cairn, then bend left for the pitched staircase of Jacob's Ladder. This descends to an old packhorse bridge, then along to some buildings (Lee Farm). Now it becomes a surfaced lane and descends to Upper Booth.

7. Cross a bridge over a stream, then turn left into a farmyard (Upper Booth). Follow the gravel drive as it bends right then through a gate. Turn left with the track following a Pennine Way sign then right following a 'Footpath to Edale' sign. The Pennine Way rises up a sandy track which fades as it begins to traverse rough pasture and fields at the foot of Broadlee-Bank Tor. At a junction below Grindslow Knoll, turn right to descend a tree-lined track to the village. Turn right along the road and back to the car park.

Where to eat and drink

The Old Nags Head or The Rambler Inn at Edale both serve bar meals, or if you prefer a café you have a choice of Newfold Farm Café by Edale Post Office or the Penny Pot Café by the station.

What to see

Along the edge of Kinder Scout's summit are peat bogs. Peat is formed by mosses such as the bright green sphagnum moss, which is now restricted to small patches. It has been replaced by sedges, grasses, heather and bilberry in a vegetation cover riven by deep and numerous haggs in which the naked peat comes to the surface. The base of the hagg has often been eroded to the gravelly surface of the core rocks. The chief reasons for this have been grazing and pollution.

While you're there

Go and visit the nearby summit of Mam Tor. Only a short (but steep) walk from the nearest road, this has a fabulous viewpoint over the whole of the Edale Valley and today's route, as well as southwards to Castleton. Bronze Age people also valued its panoramic views; look out for remnants of their hill-fort.

MAM TOR AND RUSHUP EDGE

DISTANCE/TIME	7 miles (11.3km) / 4hrs
ASCENT/GRADIENT	1,380ft (421m) / ▲ ▲ ▲
PATHS	Mainly good, but can be boggy in wet weather
LANDSCAPE	Farmland, ridgeline path, meadowland
SUGGESTED MAP	OS Explorer OL1 Peak District - Dark Peak Area
START/FINISH	Grid reference: SK124853
DOG FRIENDLINESS	Keep on lead near livestock
PARKING	Edale pay car park
PUBLIC TOILETS	Edale car park and at Moorland centre
NOTES	This area is popular with mountain bikers, so keep an eye out for them on bridleways and on the Chapel Gate track

Called the Shivering Mountain because of the instability of its shale layers, Mam Tor is the largest (and most popular) of the Peak's hill-forts and has the distinction of being the only one to be excavated. In the mid-1960s Manchester University selected Mam Tor as a training site for its archaeology students and this produced a wealth of fresh information about the fort. What can be seen today are the ramparts of a heavily fortified Iron Age settlement. The single rampart with an outer ditch and another bank can still be traced round the hillside. There were two entrances, one leading to the path from Hollins Cross and the other to the path to Mam Nick. Mam Tor was probably a partially defended site with a timber palisade that was later replaced with stone.

Ancient settlement

The excavations revealed that there had been a settlement here long before the Iron Age. Two early Bronze Age barrows were discovered on the summit, one of which the National Trust has capped in stone to make sure it is preserved. An earlier settlement on the ground enclosed by the ramparts was excavated. Here, several circular houses or huts had been built on terraced platforms on the upper slopes of the hill. The pottery and other artefacts uncovered are of a style often found in house platforms of this type and date from the late Bronze Age. Radiocarbon dating of charcoal found in the huts put them somewhere between 1700 and 1000 BC. Archaeologists G D B Jones and F H Thomson, writing about the discoveries at Mam Tor, suggested that the fort might have been built as a shelter for pastoralists using the hills for summer grazing, but decided in the end that it was more likely to have had a strategic military purpose. Depending on when it was actually built, it could have seen action during inter-tribal struggles of the native Brigantes. During a later period it may have been used as a strategic defence against the advancing Romans. Like most settlements from this far back in time, Mam Tor will probably never reveal all its secrets. However, standing on the summit and looking over the valleys, back along the path to Hollins Cross or forward to Rushup Edge, it's enough just to try to imagine the effort that went into building such a fortification with nothing but the most primitive of tools.

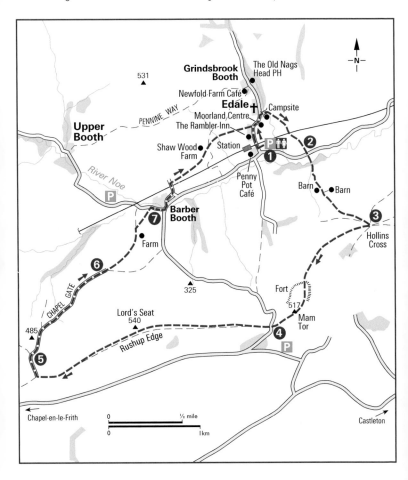

1. Exit the car park beside the public toilets and turn right on to the village road. Go under the railway bridge and past The Rambler Inn. Pass the Moorland Centre then take a footpath right by the churchyard. Cross a stream then fork right and across waymarked fields to a road – on the way, you will pass a barn and take a dirt track under the railway line.

2. Cross the road, picking up the path again which joins a farm drive. Head directly uphill past a large stone barn. As the track bends left to a second barn continue uphill, signed to Hollins Cross, then into steeper and rougher pasture, following a short section of boardwalk A steeper well-used path leads to a waymarker; the path heads more diagonally up the slope now then forks left to join a wide bridleway to Hollins Cross.

3. Fork right on a wide slabbed path which leads over the summit of Mam Tor. As you pass the summit and descend to a road, look out for small bronze castings in the stone path – these represent items that may have been common during Mam Tor's use as a fort.

4. At the road, take a few paces left then cross over to a gate. Take a broad bridleway path rising steeply on to Rushup Edge. Here, walkers head right of a fence and directly on the ridgeline – a bikers' bridleway rejoins your footpath just over a mile (1.8km) along the ridge and after four stiles. About 500yds (457m) beyond this, fork right on a wide sandy track (Chapel Gate).

5. Bend right with the main sandy track as a slabbed path forks ahead over Brown Knoll. This soon descends steeply – you may well find a narrow trod on the left is the pleasant way to descend (particularly if the track is popular with mountain bikers). Go through two gates on the descent. Immediately after the second, fork left through a walkers' gate.

6. Head diagonally right and downhill, crossing a stile and passing the remnants of two gateways between fields, then bend left beside a ruined wall to a gate. There are several stiles in the next section – follow a fence downhill to some tumbledown buildings, bend right around these, then across a farm road. Follow the continuation of the waymarked footpath to a road.

7. Turn right on to this, then left at a T-junction by a bend. Take the second left into the hamlet of Barber Booth, bend right, then turn left on a stony track signposted to Edale Station. After a railway bridge bend right and through fields. Stay left towards Edale Village at a first waymarked junction then fork right at a second (just after a farm driveway). Cross straight over the next field then continue along a field-top path to Edale. Turn right on the road to return to the car park.

Where to eat and drink

The Old Nags Head or The Rambler Inn at Edale both serve bar meals, or for a café you have a choice of Newfold Farm Café by Edale Post Office or the Penny Pot Café by the station.

What to see

On your return to Edale make sure to leave enough time to visit the fascinating Moorland Centre. Featuring interactive displays and exhibitions on ecology and wildlife of the Dark Peak moorland, the centre also provides a wet-weather shelter and toilets and has daily weather reports for walkers. Free to enter, the state-of-the-art building has a green planted roof (with sedum) and is heated by a ground source heat pump.

While you're there

The ruins of Peveril Castle at nearby Castleton are well enough preserved to give a good indication of what it looked like when it was intact. Its glorious clifftop location also gives grand views in all directions. It was built by William Peveril in 1080 after he was granted the title of Bailiff of the Royal Manors of the Peak by William I for his part in the Norman Conquest of 1066.

NAVIO ROMAN FORT AND OVER WIN HILL

DISTANCE/TIME	9.25 miles (14.9km) / 5hrs
ASCENT/GRADIENT	1,300ft (396m) / ▲ ▲ ▲
PATHS	Mainly firm field paths and hill tracks, although some slopes may be slippery after rain, many stiles
LANDSCAPE	Riverside fields and high moors and pasture
SUGGESTED MAP	OS Explorer OL1 Peak District - Dark Peak Area
START/FINISH	Grid reference: SK149829
DOG FRIENDLINESS	Dogs on lead except for enclosed tracks
PARKING	Main Castleton pay car park by visitor centre
PUBLIC TOILETS	At car park

Leaving Castleton beneath Peveril Castle's Norman keep sets the scene for a walk through history. You're treading the same ground as Roman soldiers and Celtic and Saxon warriors before you. The walk takes you on to the hillside beyond the sycamores of the River Noe. As you amble across green pastures overlooking the Hope Valley, cast your imagination back to the darker days of AD 926. Down there in the valley below you, a furious tribal battle ended in victory for King Athelstan, grandson of Alfred the Great. He would soon become the first Saxon ruler of all England.

Navio, a Roman fort
In one of those riverside fields the path comes across the earthwork remains of the Roman fort, Navio. Built in the time of Emperor Antoninus Pius, the fort stood at a junction of roads serving garrisons at Buxton, Glossop and Templeborough. At its peak it would have sheltered over 500 soldiers. It remained occupied until the 4th century, controlling the rich mining area around the Peak. Many relics from the fort are displayed at Buxton Museum.

Win Hill
Win Hill looms large in your thoughts as you cross the valley and climb towards it. As you're passing through the hamlet of Aston take a quick look at Aston Hall. Built in 1578, it has an unusual pedimented window with a weather-worn carved figure. The doorway is surrounded by Roman Doric columns and a four-centred arch. Beyond the hall the climb begins in earnest up a stony track, then through bracken and grass hillside where Win Hill's summit peeps out and spectacular views await. There are several theories on how the hill got its name. The most likely one is that it derives from an earlier name, Wythinhull, which meant Willow Hill. Another theory concerns two warlords: Edwin, the first Christian king of Northumbria, and Cuicholm, King of Wessex. Cuicholm murdered Lilla, Edwin's maidservant, and Edwin sought revenge. Cuicholm assembled his forces on Lose Hill, while Edwin camped on Win Hill. Edwin was victorious and thus his hill was named Win Hill.

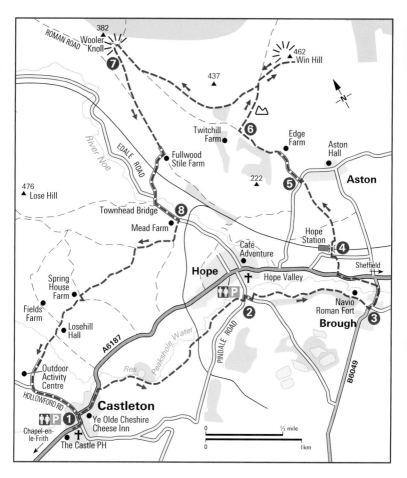

1. Turn left out of the car park and follow the main street as it winds left and right. After a quarter of a mile (400m), bear off to the right on a track signed to Hope. Beyond a farm, walk on beside Peakshole Water, shortly breaking away to cross a succession of fields. Later, after going through a small enclosed field, pass to the left of a hawthorn-topped hillock and then cross a railway line. The ongoing path leads to Pindale Road.

2. Go left and first right, leaving left after 100yds (91m) over a stile beside a gate. Head on across the field, passing through a gate to continue by the right boundary. Beyond a footbridge, cross the site of Navio Roman Fort and bear right over a final field to reach the B6049 at Brough.

3. Turn left. Immediately after the second bridge, cross a stile on the left and strike out to find a stile near the field's distant right corner. Cross the busy A6187 with care and go left, leaving just after a cottage to cross through a gate on the right. Walk along the edge of the field, then cross a stile to a footpath with a fence on the left before exiting beside some houses.

4. Walk left towards the railway station, then go right along a narrow path to a footbridge over the line. Go right to a gate and head across more

fields, keeping the hedge on your right. A contained path eventually leads out to a tarmac lane.

5. Go left and immediately right, uphill on a tarmac lane. At Edge Farm, swing left for an unsurfaced track along the top edge of a wood to a path junction above Twitchill Farm.

6. Turn right for the short ascent of Win Hill up the well-used path to the summit. From the summit trig column, leave in a westerly direction on a track (permitted footpath to Wooler Knoll) which stays on the ridgeline with fine views to both sides before passing through a gate to drop downhill and cross through a broken wall. Turn left soon after; at a path junction with a wooden waymarker.

7. Follow this path all the way to the bottom and join a lane. Turn left through a gate and continue downhill to its junction with the Edale Road. Go ahead, over Townhead Bridge, and follow the road left for just over 382yds (350m) until you reach a path on the right, just after Mead Farm and by a red post box in the wall.

8. Where the path ends, by buildings, go right towards Lose Hill on an enclosed path at the edge of a field. Fork left before a stile for a footpath signposted to Castleton that heads west to Spring House Farm. Turn left on to a lane in front of the farm, then immediatly right (signed Castleton) to walk on a track. Keep left at the junction and continue past Losehill Hall. Where the track bends left, go straight ahead on a gravelled path across fields. When it meets a rough track, turn left to pass the Outdoor Activity Centre (Hollowford Centre), then turn left on to a tarmac lane to return to Castleton.

Where to eat and drink

Castleton has numerous cafés and pubs to choose from. Further along the route, you can nip into the village of Hope which has a selection of cafés, including the popular Café Adventure on Edale Road.

What to see

Often you can see a change in the dry-stone walls. Those in the valley are made from paler limestone, while those on the Win Hill slopes are of the darker gritstone. The walls were mostly built between 1780 and 1820, when enclosure of upland areas was taking place at a prolific rate. Although expensive to build and repair, they are now considered to be an integral part of the Peakland landscape and various conservation bodies train new skilled wallers.

While you're there

The area offers a range of outdoor pursuits such as climbing, caving and mountain biking – check local adventure activity providers for taster sessions. Hope Wakes is held on the last Saturday in June, when you can see a traditional Derbyshire well dressing, and the Hope Show is held on August Bank Holiday Monday. This is a traditional agricultural show that's been held since 1853.

CASTLETON, CAVE DALE AND BLUE JOHN CAVERNS

DISTANCE/TIME	5 miles (8km) / 3hrs
ASCENT/GRADIENT	920ft (280m) / ▲ ▲
PATHS	Limestone can be slippery when wet
LANDSCAPE	Limestone ravines and high pastureland
SUGGESTED MAP	OS Explorer OL1 Peak District - Dark Peak Area
START/FINISH	Grid reference: SK149829
DOG FRIENDLINESS	Farmland; dogs should be kept on lead
PARKING	Main Castleton pay car park by visitor centre
PUBLIC TOILETS	At car park. Free public toilets also available at Treak Cliff Cavern when open

Castleton is the last settlement before the Hope Valley narrows and squeezes into the rocky ravine of Winnats. It's a bustling tourist town with a history evident back to Norman times, and a geology that has been responsible for many of its successes and most of its failures. At Castleton the shales and gritstone of the Dark Peak and the limestone plateaux of the White Peak meet. Here, countless generations of miners have dug their shafts and enlarged the natural caves that riddle the bedrock in search of precious ore. Here, too, they built an ambitious road that eventually succumbed to the landslides of Mam Tor, the 'Shivering Mountain'. The castle keep is perched high upon an outcrop of limestone. It's one of the earliest stone-built castles in the country, built shortly after the Norman Conquest by William Peveril, William the Conqueror's illegitimate son.

Dramatic caves

The entrance to Cave Dale is narrow and striking. One minute you're in the village square, the next you've turned the corner and entered an awesome limestone ravine. Geologists used to think Cave Dale was a collapsed cavern, but current thinking places it as a valley carved by glacial meltwater after the last Ice Age. A little limestone path takes you through the ravine, climbing past cave entrances and above a wide system of subterranean passages, including those of the nearby Peak Cavern. The valley shallows and the next stretch of the journey is over high green fields enclosed by dry-stone walls. Mam Tor, the Shivering Mountain, dominates the view ahead, and soon you look down on the crumbling tarmac of the ill-fated road, and the huge shale landslides that have plagued the valley for centuries.

The first Castleton cavern of the day is the superb Blue John Cavern, high on the side of Mam Tor. It takes its name from the purple-blue fluorspar, unique to Castleton. The floodlights of the chambers show off the old river galleries with crystalline waterfalls, and a fascinating array of stalagmites and stalactites. Beyond the Blue John Cavern a narrow path rakes across the steep limestone-studded slopes past Treak Cliff Cavern to the Speedwell Cavern, at the foot of the Winnats Pass. If you like boat trips, a visit to this cavern is a must. Here, lead miners excavated a level into the hill through which they built a subterranean canal, 547yds (500m) long. This took them 11 years, but low yields and high costs forced the early closure of the mine. The fascinating boat trip takes you down the canal to a landing stage just short of the 'Bottomless Pit', named because the spoil thrown in by miners made no impression on its depth.

The last stretch takes you across the National Trust's Long Cliff Estate. Before retreating to Castleton, take one last look back up the valley, and across the limestone that was once a coral reef in a tropical lagoon.

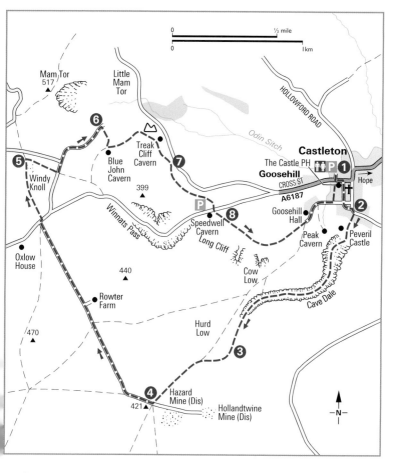

1. From the car park turn left up the main street and then right to walk along Castle Street, passing the church on your way. Bend left then right with the road through Market Place leaving the small triangular green on your left and rising to the start of Pindale Road.

2. As the road bends left, turn off right between cottages into Cave Dale. Through a gate, the path enters the narrow limestone gorge, overlooked by the

ruined keep of Peveril Castle perched on the cliffs above to the right. As you gain height, the gorge shallows and passes through a wall via a gateless gateway and a track joins from the right near a permissive access path.

3. Continue uphill to a gate in a dry-stone wall at plateau level, and follow the well-defined path across high pastureland. It passes through a gate in another wall before being joined by a path from the right at an oblique waymarked junction. Follow the waymarker diagonally left on a wide but fainter track over the crest of a rise, now heading for a gate in the far corner of the field. A short-walled passage leads out to a broad track near the old Hazard Mine.

4. Turn right through a gate along a stony walled track, which shortly swings right and then runs straight for a mile (1.6km) past Rowter Farm to meet a road near Oxlow House. Cross to a gate on a dog-leg right across the road and follow a stony track past the rise of Windy Knoll, once quarried for its stone.

5. After a quarter of a mile (400m), just past the rise of Windy Knoll, turn right on a faint path back to the road. Go left and then fork right along the old Mam Tor Road, signed 'Blue John Cavern'.

6. Turn in at the entrance to the cave and swing left in front of the ticket office to a gate. Follow a path to a second gate, from which the way drops around the shoulder of the hill and on towards Treak Cliff Cavern. Go left down the concrete steps by the ticket office, then right on a path with handrails.

7. Part-way down, bear right through a gap to follow a path across the hillside. Where the path forks beyond a stile, bear right to come out on the Winnats Pass road by Speedwell Cavern.

8. A path opposite takes the route on to the National Trust's Long Cliff Estate. Keep beside the wall as it later curves left below Cow Low, shortly leaving the fields to join the end of a street. Walk down past cottages, cross Goosehill Bridge and turn left on a streamside path that leads out to the main road opposite the car park.

Where to eat and drink
To complete your round-up of all the local places containing the word 'castle', try the 17th-century Castle in Castle Street, which serves food daily and has an outside garden area. For a café, try the Three Roofs Café or Rose Cottage, both on Cross Street.

What to see
Treak Cliff Cavern is one of the best places to see fossils. In the limestone you can study the remains of sea creatures that accumulated in the bed of a tropical sea 320 million years ago.

While you're there
Besides the caverns seen en route, try to make time for Peveril Castle, looked after by English Heritage. It has a well-preserved Norman keep and also offers wonderful views up Cave Dale and over the village.

HATHERSAGE TO STANAGE

16

DISTANCE/TIME	9.5 miles (15.3km) / 5hrs
ASCENT/GRADIENT	1,700ft (518m) / ▲▲
PATHS	Well-defined paths and tracks, several stiles
LANDSCAPE	Gritstone and heather moorland
SUGGESTED MAP	OS Explorer OL1 Peak District - Dark Peak Area
START/FINISH	Grid reference: SK232814
DOG FRIENDLINESS	Dogs are banned from northwestern part of Stanage Edge (beyond High Neb) due to nesting birds; elsewhere keep on lead
PARKING	Pay car park, Oddfellows Road, Hathersage
PUBLIC TOILETS	Main road, Hathersage, and on lane above North Lees

From Moscar, to Baslow a line of dark cliffs caps the heather moors east of the Derwent Valley. Writer Daniel Defoe called it a vast extended moor or waste in which strangers would be obliged to take guides or lose their way. Later, Charlotte Brontë visited Hathersage when staying with her friend Ellen Nussey, the wife of the local vicar. She would have found the place much more acceptable and not unlike her home at Haworth.

In the 1890s, the climber J W Putrell turned to the highest of these cliffs, Stanage Edge, and pioneered several gully routes. Others would follow and today Stanage and its neighbouring 'edges' are one of the most popular climbing venues in Britain. But Stanage is a great place for walkers too, for they can stride out on firm skyline paths with Sheffield on one side and Derbyshire on the other. High car parks mean that you can walk Stanage without much ascent, but it's more rewarding to work for your fun, so this route starts at Hathersage.

Hathersage is located by the banks of the River Derwent. The route starts gently on Baulk Lane and passes the cricket ground on its way through the little valley of Hood Brook. Gradients steepen and the route comes across the 16th-century castellated manor of North Lees Hall, the inspiration for Thornfield Hall, Mr Rochester's home in *Jane Eyre* (written by Charlotte Brontë after staying in the area). The Eyre family did exist in real life and, at the time of her visits, were living in the Hall.

Above the hall the route climbs on to the moors and a paved causeway takes it to the top of the cliffs. The cliff-edge path to High Neb and Crow Chin is a delight and the views from it are extensive. After rejoining the edge, the path passes above Robin Hood's Cave, where the legendary outlaw perhaps hid from the Sheriff of Nottingham, to reach the high road and the climbers' car park. Now there's just Higger Tor to do. The rocky knoll surrounded by an ocean of heather makes a fine finale, one last lofty perch before the descent back to Hathersage.

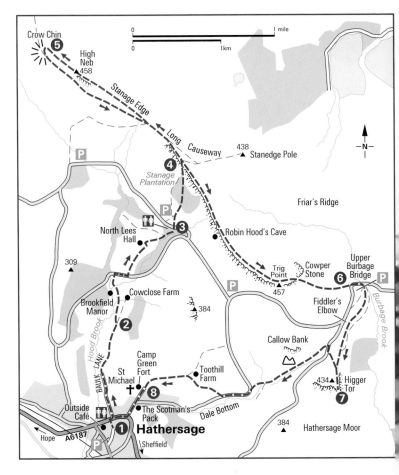

1. Leave the bottom of the car park along a path leading to Main Street. Turn right, then left into Baulk Lane. On leaving town, it degrades to a track before winding away between open fields.

2. After 0.75 miles (1.2km), at a fork near Cowclose Farm, bear left to a gate. Skirt Brookfield Manor to emerge on a tarmac lane (Birley Lane). Go right, but leave after 200yds (183m) along a track on the left. Pass around North Lees Hall, then turn right up steps to another track. Follow it across a meadow into a wood. Towards the top, a path branches left up steps to a tarmac lane near toilets.

3. Cross to a path opposite, climbing through bracken into Stanage Plantation. Emerging at the top, keep with the path ahead, rising between boulders on to the edge.

4. Follow the path left to join a track, the Long Causeway. After 50yds (46m) branch right to regain the edge and continue for a mile (1.6km), passing the trig column on High Neb to Crow Chin, a little further on.

5. Just before the edge swings north, take an obvious path clambering down to a broad grass track that once served the quarries. Return beneath the cliffs, eventually rejoining the Long Causeway. Follow it back up to the edge. Leave at an access waymarker to continue along the clifftop path over a ranch stile. After half a mile (800m), a narrow path drops down to Robin Hood's Cave. Return to the edge and carry on to another trig column at the end of the ridge.

6. The onward path descends across the moor to a tarmac road. Turn left on the road, walking to a car park and leaving it through a kissing gate. Take the higher of the two paths to Higger Tor.

7. From the rocky top, turn sharp right down to the tarmac lane. Cross diagonally to a stile. Walk forward 20yds (18m) to a cross-path and turn left, descending below Callow Bank. Go through a gate and keep ahead on a rough track, which shortly leads to another tarmac lane. Go left for a quarter of a mile (400m) before leaving right on a track (no sign). As buildings appear, pass through a gate on the left and angle down below Toothill Farm across a couple of rough fields. Meet the line of a sunken path and follow it downhill to cross over a stile to another sunken path amongst trees, meeting a tarmac lane. Continue downhill as it winds past houses and cuts through Camp Green, a medieval camp, before passing a lane leading to the church.

8. On meeting School Lane, turn right to the main road, going right again into the village. Turn in at the gates of the Methodist Church and go back to the car park.

Where to eat and drink
Hathersage has a selection of cafés including Coleman's Deli and the renowned Outside Café located on the upstairs floor of the Outside Shop. The Scotsman's Pack, on School Lane, is an old coaching inn with outside seating by a stream and two dining areas for meals. There's often a snack van in the car park at Upper Burbage Bridge.

What to see
Beneath the cliffs of Stanage Edge you'll see piles of old millstones and grindstones, some intact and some incomplete. They are the abandoned relics of an industry that supplied the flourishing steelworks of Sheffield and local corn mills. French imports, which were both cheaper and better, and the coming of the roller mills saw the decline of the industry by the 1860s.

While you're there
The parish church of St Michael, just off the route above the village, dates back to the 14th century. By the south door of the church is a grave claimed to be that of Robin Hood's henchman, Little John. Back in the centre of the village, near the car park, is an outdoor swimming pool which is open from May to October.

BURBAGE EDGE AND CARL WARK

DISTANCE/TIME	5.75 miles (9.2km) / 3hrs 30min
ASCENT/GRADIENT	900ft (274m) / ▲ ▲
PATHS	Generally good paths, although moorland path below Carl Wark may be indistinct and boggy in wet weather, no stiles
LANDSCAPE	Millstone tors and quarries, heather moors and woodland
SUGGESTED MAP	OS Explorer OL1 Peak District - Dark Peak Area
START/FINISH	Grid reference: SK252801
DOG FRIENDLINESS	Keep on lead near sheep, particularly at lambing time and from March to July
PARKING	Surprise View pay car park on A6187 east of Hathersage
PUBLIC TOILETS	None on route

On the moors beyond Hathersage, history and geology combine to produce a fascinating panorama. The main stone bed from which this area is formed is Chatsworth grit, a coarse sandstone with scattered pebbles, that is extremely resistant to erosion. This was once much valued as a building material and many Peak District buildings, including Chatsworth House, are constructed from it. Its other major use was to fashion grinding stones for the emerging Sheffield tool and cutlery industry and to provide millstones for grinding corn. Millstone Edge was once a thriving quarrying area. However, the introduction of carborundum (a synthetic abrasive) in the 20th century led to a fall in demand for millstone grit and the consequent demise of the quarrying industry. You can still see piles of half-fashioned millstones lying amidst the debris of quarried stone near the start of this walk.

The escarpment that forms Burbage Edge is an impressive backdrop for a series of flat-topped hills rising from the moor. Over Owler Tor, Winyards Nick, Higger Tor and Carl Wark were once part of the same sandstone bed as Burbage Edge but were displaced by faulting. With their concave sides, bare gritstone edges and level surfaces, these uplands were ideal sites for fortification. There are at least nine examples of hill-forts in the Peak District probably dating from the Iron Age, and Carl Wark is certainly one of the most spectacular. It is defended naturally on all but one of its sides by very steep slopes; on the undefended side a stone rampart has been built, about 20ft (6m) wide at the base with boulders bonded to a wall of turf. In the southwest corner, where the defensive wall turns inwards, lies what would once have been the fort's entrance. The age of the fort has never been confirmed. Some place it in the post-Roman period of the 5th and 6th centuries AD because of the technique used in building the stone and turf wall, and because of similarities with the construction of Dark Age (AD 500–1100) forts in Scotland. Others have argued that the 'in-turned' entrance suggests a much earlier Iron Age construction. Gardom's Edge, near Baslow to the south, which is similar to Carl Wark in that its interior is small and rocky with little space for buildings, is actually a neolithic enclosure; however, nothing has yet been found at Carl Wark to date it to this time. It is likely that Carl Wark was originally an Iron or Bronze Age construction which was refortified by the Romans.

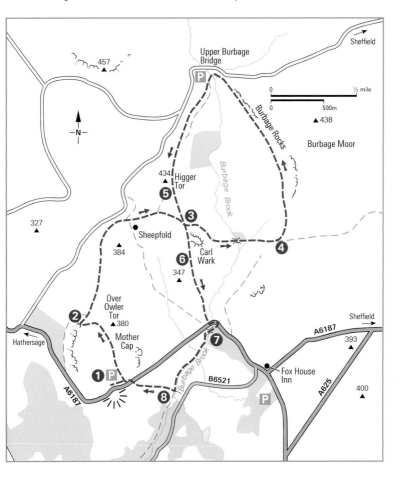

1. Leave the car park through a kissing gate opposite the entrance, rising towards birch wood. Walk on, veering right and clambering up rocks to a crossing path. Go left, with the prominent outcrop of Mother Cap soon appearing. Pass to its left and continue towards Over Owler Tor. Just before the outcrop, head down left on a narrower path, crossing the heather to meet a path beside a fence.

2. Turn right along the path, which later leaves the fence and continues straight ahead to contour the hillside towards distant Higger Tor, eventually reaching a wall on the left. Where that turns away, fork right and then, passing a clump of trees, go right again on a fainter path. Walk on, joining another wall

on your right. The path fragments to avoid boggy patches, but keep heading to the left corner of Carl Wark, now ahead.

3. Ignore a crossing path and descend below the northern flank of Carl Wark. The path again splinters, but head towards the right corner of a small pine wood, where a packhorse bridge crosses Burbage Brook. Continue forwards to cross a second stream, rising beyond to reach a broad track.

4. Follow the track left to Upper Burbage Bridge, crossing the tributary streams below the road. Head to a kissing gate by the car park, turning left before it along the higher of two paths, which leads to Higger Tor. Climb to the top and continue left along the plateau to descend from the southeast corner, picking through rocks.

5. Follow the path across the moor towards Carl Wark. Climb to the massive defensive wall and turn in to explore the summit plateau. Leave through the original defensive gateway at the other end of the wall and descend south across more moss.

6. The path becomes clearer, rising over the flank of a lesser hill, then falling beyond to the A6187. Cross this busy road with care and go left over a bridge (no pavement), leaving through a gate on the right into woodland.

7. Bear right at a fork, crossing a bubbling stream, then over a footbridge across Burbage Brook. Follow the riverside path downstream.

8. At the next bridge, turn sharp right up a sunken path through the heath, which ends at the road opposite the car park. Turn left on the road and cross with care to arrive back at the car park.

Where to eat and drink
The Millstone Inn is on the A6187 between the car park and Hathersage. A former coaching inn, it has been serving the needs of travellers since the 19th century. The pub has open fires, traditional cask ales and food using locally sourced produce. The Fox House Inn is towards Sheffield, not far from Burbage Bridge.

What to see
The elegant stone bridge across Burbage Brook is a fine example of a packhorse bridge. It was erected around 1750 to avoid the difficulties of fording the stream in flood, although the route between Houndkirk Moor and Hathersage on which it stands is far older. The bridge was wide enough to allow the single-file passage of pack animals and was built without parapets so it wouldn't obstruct the loaded side panniers they carried.

While you're there
To find out more about Carl Wark and many other prehistoric sites around the Peak District, it's worth making a trip into nearby Sheffield, where the Weston Park Museum has an extensive collection of finds from the area. There are also displays about the ecology and climate of the Peak District, alongside exhibitions reflecting Sheffield's industrial past, particularly its role in the manufacture of cutlery.

CRACKEN EDGE
AND SOUTH HEAD

DISTANCE/TIME	6 miles (9.7km) / 3hrs 30min
ASCENT/GRADIENT	1,380ft (421m) / ▲ ▲ ▲
PATHS	Field paths, quarry and farm tracks, sandy and eroded around quarry, several stiles
LANDSCAPE	Hill pastures, long-abandoned quarry and moorland
SUGGESTED MAP	OS Explorer OL1 Peak District - Dark Peak Area
START/FINISH	Grid reference: SK040827
DOG FRIENDLINESS	Dogs should be kept on lead
PARKING	Roadside parking at start near war memorial
PUBLIC TOILETS	None on route
NOTES	Path to Cracken Edge is getting eroded may not be suitable for all. Beware crag edges along top. Alternatively take a slightly lower path below the crags (both described)

The best base for exploring both of these hills is Chinley. Two sweeping curved viaducts that span the valley high above the town's rooftops are a reminder that this was once an important railway town: a junction for Sheffield, Manchester and Derby trains. The Reverend Henry Thorald called the viaducts one of the greatest monuments to Victorian industrial England. At one time over 150 trains a day would have raced through the valley. At its height Chinley station had a café, a bookstall and bustling waiting rooms on every platform.

On leaving Chinley you are confronted by the rust-coloured crags known as Cracken Edge. They form the upper of two distinct tiers. When you get closer the crags turn out to be the remains of old gritstone quarries. Further exploration reveals the entrances of shafts dug to extract the best stone; later on, part of the winding engine that conveyed the stone down to the valley below comes into sight. Today the scene is one of nature reclaiming industry, with grassed-over spoil heaps and narrow wash-out valleys.

When you reach the brow of Cracken Edge you're rewarded with a panorama of the second part of the walk. In it, Kinder Scout peeps over the grassy peaks of Mount Famine and South Head. A pleasant grass track takes the route down from the edge back to the fields of Otter Brook's upper combe. At Chinley Head you come to a stark stone-built house called Peep-O-Day, so named as it faces eastwards and catches the first of the morning sunshine. These days, privacy hedging means the small eye-shaped window built to catch those early sunrays is hard to spot. The second part of the walk is spent on the eastern side of the combe of the Otter Brook. Another substantial old quarry track takes the route across the lower slopes of Mount Famine to a windswept little pass beneath South Head. From here the Sett Valley and the attractive field patterns surrounding South Head Farm are hidden by the gritstone rim of Mount Famine and the woods of Kinder Bank. The highland plateau of Kinder Scout has disappeared behind the spur of Kinderlow End. But it's only a short climb to the summit of South Head at 1,620ft (494m) to bring it all back into view, and much more, before ending the day with an easy descent back into the valley below using farm tracks and field paths.

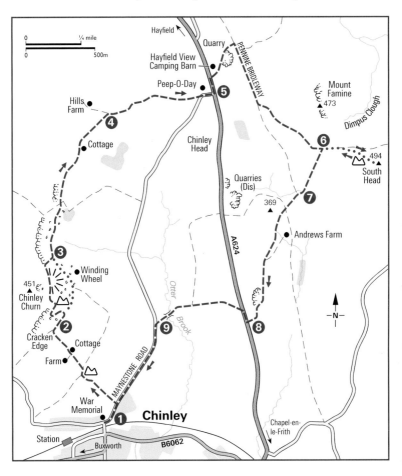

1. From the war memorial by the railway bridge, walk up Maynestone Road. After 200yds (183m), take a waymarked path on the left. Cross a stile and climb directly uphill, then diagonally left by gorse to the top left field corner. Turn right on to a vehicle track, then fork left at a junction and past a cattle grid. Where the track bends left towards buildings, continue straight ahead on a grassy path. Pass a cottage, then roughly follow the left wall in the next field. A narrow eroding track then leads steeply uphill through gorse.

2. On leveller ground, turn right on to a wider track through ancient quarry workings. About 100yds (91m) before a fence, fork left to zigzag up the hillside through higher workings. Turn right below the edge-top to a stile. For the best views, head left along the fenceline to the top of the edge then bear right carefully along a faint crag-edge path. Bend right with the edge to descend a gentle ramp to rejoin the lower path. Otherwise continue on the path ahead, weaving through the spoil heaps below the crags.

3. As the paths rejoin, bend gently right then left through a grassy line of spoil to pick up a broader plateau-edge path. Head left along this, past further workings. The path broadens into a track as it falls beyond a cottage to a track junction.

4. Turn right on a farm track (from Hills Farm) and descend to a lane, continuing past the evocatively named Peep-O-Day to the A624.

5. Cross over and walk left along the verge of the busy road. At Hayfield View camping barn, bear right on to the old cart track and past a small quarry. Join the Pennine Bridleway towards South Head at a T-junction. Bend left up to a pair of gates and continue beside the right-hand wall across the slope of Mount Famine to a gate on to National Trust land.

6. For the view from South Head, follow the ongoing track to an old gateway, where a grassy path branches up to the summit. Otherwise scale the stile immediately before the National Trust gate; head downfield beside the left wall and then along a walled track.

7. Cross a stile and stay near the left wall, crossing over a track junction between fields. A grass track then develops to join a farm access track (from Andrews Farm).

8. Cross the busy A624, ignore a footpath immediately opposite and follow the pavement right for about 100yds (91m). Cross a waymarked stile and bear diagonally right to the far field corner. Carry on at the edge of two more fields towards Otter Brook. Bear left just above the stream to cross a slabbed bridge.

9. Climb left from the trees to a gate at the top of the field on to Maynestone Road. Turn left back to the war memorial.

Where to eat and drink
The Navigation Inn at Buxworth is a cosy little pub with seafaring memorabilia and historical photos on the walls. Its menu consists mainly of traditional, home-cooked meals.

What to see
At the top of Maynestones Lane, opposite Summerfield, look out for an impressive owl carved in a tall tree stump.

While you're there
Have a look around Buxworth, a village a mile (1.6km) or so west of Chinley. This was once a busy inland port and a terminus for the Peak Forest Tramway and the Peak Forest Canal. These pre-railway industrial transport routes were built in 1806 to link the Peak District with the River Mersey.

AROUND LYME PARK

DISTANCE/TIME	5.2 miles (8.4km) / 3hrs
ASCENT/GRADIENT	855ft (260m) / ▲ ▲
PATHS	Generally firm, field tracks can be boggy if wet, several stiles
LANDSCAPE	Rolling parkland and fields, some moorland
SUGGESTED MAP	OS Explorer OL1 Peak District – Dark Peak Area
START/FINISH	Grid reference: SJ962823
DOG FRIENDLINESS	Keep on lead in park and near livestock; under close control at all other times
PARKING	Lyme Park, off A6 (free to National Trust members, charge at entrance to non-members)
PUBLIC TOILETS	By Timber Yard Café, near main car park
NOTES	Lyme Park opening hours: 8–8 summer, 8–6 winter

Lyme Park was originally created by Richard II, who, in 1398, granted land in the Royal Forest of Macclesfield. It became the ancestral home of the Legh family for the next five and a half centuries, and they were responsible for developing the original house into the sumptuous pile that you see today. In 1946 the house and park were donated to the National Trust. The grounds are open all year and the lovely rolling parkland and moorland tracks with their fabulous views over Cheshire and the Dark Peak are well worth exploring.

It's the classic English stately home: a medieval manor house that was gradually transformed into a large and elegant Palladian mansion, and which is today full of antique furniture and tapestries, carvings and clocks. Outside, there are formal gardens (including an Edwardian Rose Garden and an Orangery), plus 1,400 acres (567ha) of gorgeous open moorland and parkland that are home to herds of red and fallow deer. Such is the sheer magnetism of the place that it was chosen to be the location of Pemberley for BBC Television's adaptation of Jane Austen's *Pride and Prejudice* in 1995, and the sight of a wet Mr Darcy (played by Colin Firth) striding across the grounds remains indelibly printed on many minds.

Near Pursefield Wood is the 300-year-old Paddock Cottage, which was built partly to enhance the radiating views visitors enjoyed to and from the main house. A few of these so-called vista lines, all carefully plotted so that the house can be admired from surrounding locations, are still visible today, including one impressive corridor through the trees of Knightslow Wood to the south of the house.

Other eye-catching buildings include the various lodges that are dotted around the park's perimeter, including Parkgate Lodge. This was once known as the Dower House and was where the widowed mothers of the Lords of the Manor would be expected to reside. Although the house is often hidden by the undulating moorland and dense patches of woodland, this walk offers ever-changing views of Lyme Park, from tree-lined avenues and open meadows to the tiny reservoirs of the Bollinhurst Valley.

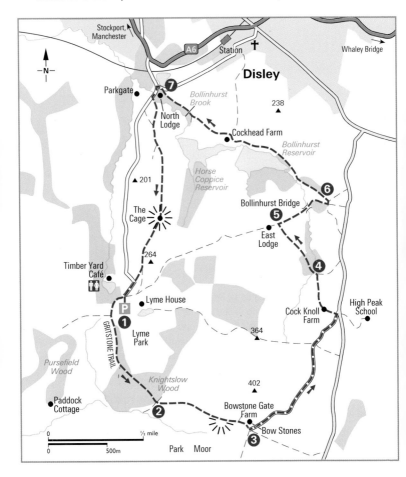

1. With the information booth behind you, cross the main car park then turn left up the main drive. Just before it bends over a cattle grid, fork off left along a broad track, towards Knightslow Wood, and follow this ahead through a gate. The trail climbs beside a long stand of pine trees. Pass through another gate into the wood and take the left fork.

2. On reaching a gate at the far side, take the track ahead, which snakes on to the moor towards communication masts sprouting from the skyline. Go over a ladder stile near the top then emerge at the top of a lane by Bowstone Gate Farm. (The Bow Stones themselves are set back in a small enclosure to the left of the lane just beyond the farm entrance.)

3. Turn left and follow the lane downhill to a junction opposite the entrance to High Peak School. Turn left immediately up a farm drive (Cock Knoll Farm)

signed to East Lodge. Bear right through the farmyard, leaving through a gate by the end barn. Head straight down the left-hand side of the field.

4. By a small patch of woodland, fork left through a metal gate then across a stream. Bend right just beyond a set of ruins under some tall beech trees, then occasional waymarkers guide you across several rough pastures to emerge over a stile on to a track (the main Gritstone Trail route)

5. A shortcut leads left past East Lodge to Lyme House, but the main route turns right and down to the unsafe Bollinhurst Bridge. This is now bypassed by a wooden footbridge, then climb past a Millennium Woodland to a junction of paths.

6. Go left through a gate and head left (signed North Lodge) across a rough meadow. Descend gently beside a wood on the right, shortly crossing a stile. Continue on a narrow wooded spur between two streams, crossing the right-most stream by a stone wall then over a stile. Continue beside the wall, soon at the edge of pastures overlooking Bollinhurst Reservoir. Cross over a track then continue ahead through fields just right of a farm. Go right over a stile into woodland and follow a wide track above a small ravine. Turn right at a junction and carry on along tarmac to a park entrance (North Lodge).

7. Turn left through the lodge gate and left again along the main park drive. Almost immediately, fork left then follow intermittent red arrow waymarkers on to the hill, along its spine past the grand hilltop building 'The Cage', then down towards Lyme House. Approaching the ornamental gates, a track on the right drops back to the car park.

Where to eat and drink

There is a wide variety of cafés within Lyme Park, from the Ale Cellar Restaurant inside the house which serves a range of 'traditional meals and historic menus' and is licensed, to an ice-cream kiosk by the information centre. The Timber Yard Café, located near the car park by the large millpond, is relaxed and informal with plenty of indoor and outdoor seating and a decent range of snacks and light refreshments.

What to see

The curious hilltop tower known as The Cage is one of Lyme Park's most visible landmarks. An elegant three-storey building, it was built around 1735 as a banqueting house, but since then has been used as an observation tower, as a lodging for the park's gamekeepers, and even as a temporary prison for poachers. After falling derelict it has undergone restoration and is occasionally open.

While you're there

The nearby Macclesfield Canal forms part of the Cheshire Ring Canal Walk, a 97-mile (156km) circular route around Greater Manchester incorporating the towpaths of six historic canals, including the Peak Forest and the Trent & Mersey. The stretch past Lyme Park, between Macclesfield and Marple, is rural and peaceful.

20 COMBS AND COMBS RESERVOIR

DISTANCE/TIME	4 miles (6.4km) / 2hrs 30min
ASCENT/GRADIENT	500ft (152m) / ▲ ▲
PATHS	Can be muddy, several stiles
LANDSCAPE	Reservoir, meadows and high moors
SUGGESTED MAP	OS Explorer OL1 Peak District - Dark Peak Area
START/FINISH	Grid reference: SK034798
DOG FRIENDLINESS	Farmland; dogs should be kept on lead
PARKING	Combs Reservoir car park
PUBLIC TOILETS	None on route

This is a fine little corner of Derbyshire, tucked away from the crowds of Castleton and Hathersage. The route starts by the west side of the dam on a narrow path between the reservoir and Meveril Brook. The site is an SSSI due to a community of short-lived mosses and liverworts. The reservoir itself feeds the Peak Forest Canal and has a sailing club based on it. You may see great crested grebes swimming among the rushes. Beyond the reservoir the path tucks under the railway, which brings to mind a mysterious story concerning Ned Dixon, who lived in nearby Tunstead Farm. Ned, or Dickie as he was known, was brutally murdered by his cousin. Locals say his spirit lived on in his skull, which was left outside to guard against intruders. Strange things were said to happen when anybody tried to remove the skull. It is also claimed that the present road from Combs to Chapel was constructed because the railway bridge would not stand over Dane Hey Road. After the first bridge was completed it collapsed, burying the workmen's tools. This was blamed on the skull: Dickie had been against the railway going across Tunstead land.

Combs

A lane with hedges of honeysuckle and hawthorn winds into the village of Combs, where a handful of stone-built cottages are centred on the welcoming Beehive Inn. Combs' most famous son is Herbert Froode. He made his name in automotive engineering as one of the inventors of the brake lining. Starting out in the early 1890s he developed woven cotton brakes for horse-drawn wagons, but his ideas didn't really take off until 1897 when the first motor buses emerged. Froode applied his knowledge of brakes to this much greater challenge and by the end of the century had won a contract to supply brake linings for the new London omnibuses. Ferodo, his company, is an anagram of his surname.

Final views

Through the village the route takes to the hillsides. Now Combs Reservoir, which is spread beneath your feet, looks every bit a natural lake. Beyond it are the plains of Manchester and the hazy blue West Pennine horizon. In the other direction the gritstone cliffs of Combs Edge, which look rather like those of Kinder Scout, overshadow the sullen combe of Pyegreave Brook. This very pleasing walk ends as it starts, by the shores of the reservoir. If you look along the line of the dam towards the right of two farms, you'll see where Dickie lived. He's probably watching you, too.

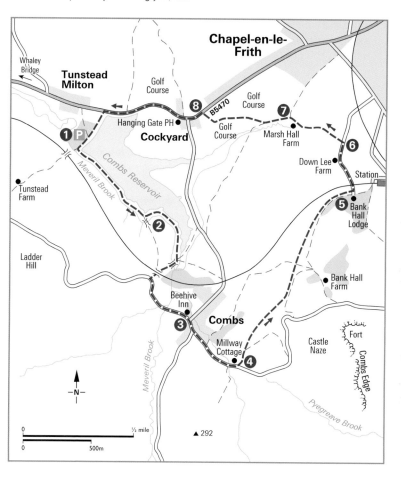

1. Follow the path from the dam along the reservoir's western shore, ignoring the first footbridge over Meveril Brook.

2. As the reservoir narrows the path traverses small fields, then comes to another footbridge over the brook. This time cross it and head straight across another field. Beyond a foot tunnel under the Buxton Line railway, the path reaches a narrow hedge-lined country lane. Turn left along the lane into Combs village.

3. Past the Beehive Inn in the village centre, take the lane straight ahead, then the left fork. This climbs out of the village towards Combs Edge.

4. Take the second footpath on the left, which begins at a muddy clearing just beyond Millway Cottage. Go through the gate and climb on a partially slabbed path and then uphill across pasture with the wall on your right. Away to the

right is the huge combe of Pyegreave Brook with Castle Naze on its left. Head uphill following the wall. Go through a gap in the boundary wall that once would have been a gate and continue uphill before crossing the remains of an old boundary wall. Head for the right end of the remains of the next boundary wall. Continue across the field and go over a stile, continuing straight ahead with a wall on your right. When the path forks, keep right to the higher path by a wall, looking down on to a sunken path. Cross another stile and keep ahead, with the railway line and reservoir below and to the left.

5. The path comes down to a track that runs alongside the railway line. This joins a lane just short of Bank Hall Lodge. Turn left to go under the railway and north to Down Lee Farm.

6. Turn left through a kissing gate 100yds (91m) beyond the farmhouse. Cross a field and stile to walk with a line of trees and fence on your right, towards Marsh Hall Farm. The fields can become very boggy on the final approaches. When you reach the farm complex turn right through a gate and follow a vehicle track heading northwest.

7. After 109yds (100m), turn left over a stile and immediately right through a gate on to a field path alongside the edge of Chapel-en-le-Frith Golf Course. Crossing over a stile on to the golf course, waymarking arrows show the path across the fairway. The stile marking the exit from the golf course is on the right (grid ref SK044799) before reaching the clubhouse. Cross a small field to reach the B5470.

8. Turn left along the road (there's a pavement on the far side), and follow it past the Hanging Gate pub at Cockyard. After passing the entrance to the sailing club, turn left to cross over the dam of Combs Reservoir and return to the car park.

Where to eat and drink
The walk has two pubs en route: the Beehive Inn at Combs and the Hanging Gate on the B5470 at Cockyard. Further afield, visit Chapel-en-le-Frith to find a wider selection of cafés and pubs.

What to see
Castle Naze (also known as Combs Moss) on Combs Edge is an old hill-fort covering approximately 2.25 acres (0.9ha) and dating back to the Iron Age period. It is protected on the western side by cliffs of up to 52ft (16m) high which were popular with climbers in the early 1900s.

While you're there
Take a look around charming Chapel-en-le-Frith (Chapel in the Forest), a traditional market town with a cobbled square and the 14th-century church of St Thomas Becket. In 1648, 1,500 Scottish soldiers were taken prisoner and locked in the church after the Battle of Ribbleton Moor; 44 soldiers died in what was to be known as the Black Hole of Derbyshire. Chapel-en-le-Frith holds a traditional carnival in June and has a range of independent shops and award-winning cafés.

TO WHITE NANCY ABOVE BOLLINGTON

DISTANCE/TIME	4.4 miles (7.1km) / 2hrs 30min
ASCENT/GRADIENT	715ft (218m) / ▲ ▲
PATHS	Field paths and farm tracks, roadside pavement, one short, sharp descent
LANDSCAPE	Mostly gentle rolling pasture and small pockets of woodland
SUGGESTED MAP	OS Explorer OL24 Peak District – White Peak Area
START/FINISH	Grid reference: SJ936779
DOG FRIENDLINESS	Under close control, on lead through farmland
PARKING	Pool Bank free car park, on Palmerston Road
PUBLIC TOILETS	Adlington Road car park, In car park

Bollington lies just outside the far western edge of the Peak District National Park, but it continues to attract walkers and sightseers due in part to the short but inviting ridge of Kerridge Hill that overlooks the small Cheshire town. However, it's not just the superb views that will hold your attention, but also the curiously shaped monument that occupies the far northern tip of the hill.

White Nancy, standing at 920ft (280m) above sea level, is a round stone construction that was built by the local Gaskell family in 1820 to commemorate the Battle of Waterloo. It was originally an open shelter with a stone table and benches, and was presumably a popular spot for picnics, but gradual decay and occasional vandalism led to it being bricked up, and now the building has no discernible door or windows, nor does it bear any plaque or information panel. Most striking of all, it is painted bright white. In terms of shape it resembles a large bell, or perhaps a giant chess pawn, with a large base that tapers into an odd little point. As for its name, the most entertaining version suggests that Nancy was the name of one of the eight horses that pulled the heavy stone table to the summit when the tower was built. Beacons are still lit next to it to mark special occasions.

Stone quarries

For all its scenic qualities, the lower western slopes of Kerridge Hill are still quarried, although this isn't visible on the walk until you reach the main summit ridge. The dressed stone is used for roofing slates and paving slabs and originally it was removed via narrow boats on the Macclesfield Canal which also served the mills and factories that once dotted the Bollington area. For a while shallow pits in the hill even yielded enough coal to supply the local engine houses, as steam power replaced water power during the Industrial Revolution's relentless advance. But inevitably your eye will be drawn to sights further afield, and if the weather is clear there will be good views across Macclesfield and the Cheshire Plain to the Mersey Estuary and the urban sprawl of Manchester, as well as the outline of the Pennines away to the north.

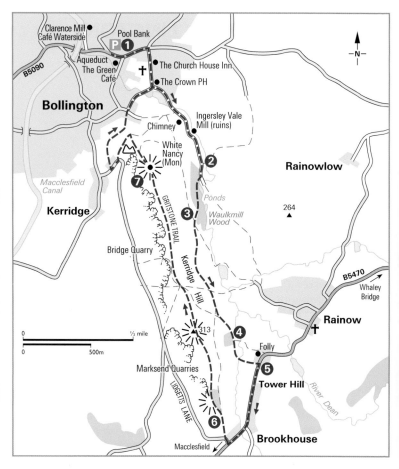

1. From the car park, turn left up the main road, then right at a roundabout on to Church Street. Turn left outside The Crown pub into Ingersley Vale. Rise up past some industrial buildings and as the bank to the right becomes a low grit-stone crag, look up above it for a tall chimney. This used to serve the Ingersley Vale Mill, the ruins of which become visible just over a slight crest in the road.

2. Rise gently up the lane to a fork by some terraced cottages on your right, go right here. The weir and pond soon below on your left would once have fed the Ingersley Vale Mill. The lane then becomes a cool and shady path through the Woodland Trust's Waulkmill Wood.

3. Leave the wood via a kissing gate and take a slabbed path across two sloping fields. The path briefly detours right and uphill around some buildings, then on through hillside fields, eventually crossing under a power line.

4. In the next field, fork left on a grassy path. Pass through a gate to run along the bottom edge of a new, mixed plantation, then through a gate and a wood-land path to a walled track to reach the main road at Tower Hill.

5. Detour briefly left to see the folly of Tower Hill; for the main route, turn right and walk along the pavement for half a mile (805m). Turn sharp right into Lidgetts Lane.

6. As it bends almost immediately left, go straight ahead through a metal gate. Then go on to a gated track past a row of hawthorn trees. After another gate, fork to the left and follow this path up to the ridge above. Ignore the lower route by the right-hand fence.

7. After admiring the views at the monument (White Nancy), with Bollington spread out below, drop sharply down the pitched path beyond, then turn left on to a sunken concrete farm lane, descending to a lane on a bend. Turn right, then almost immediately turn right again on to a footpath which soon becomes a gently descending slabbed path. Fork left with the slabbed path into fields at a path junction, descending more steeply to a road junction at the top of Lord Street. Head steeply down Lord Street then retrace your steps from The Crown to the start.

Where to eat and drink

Bollington is quite a sprawling town with no obvious centre, but it has a very wide choice of pubs, as well as a couple of cafés and a bakery on the main road (B5090). One pub renowned for good food is The Church House Inn near the bottom of Church Street; alternatively, The Green, a café on High Street is a café with a growing reputation.

What to see

In the mid-1800s there were as many as 13 mills in Bollington, spinning cotton and silk, and later synthetic fibres such as rayon. The last cotton mill closed in 1960, but some of the town's surviving mill buildings have a new lease of life as modern offices and flats. On the walk, look out for the ruins of the Ingersley Vale silk mill, whose waterwheel was one of the largest in England. Now look further up the lane on your right to a high embankment; this is the line of the former leat coming into the mill – you will see the intake pools further along the route.

While you're there

Another fascinating throwback to a previous industrial age is the impressive Telford-designed aqueduct, which carries the Macclesfield Canal high above the main road through Bollington. There's also a café in the former mill building beside it (Clarence Mill). Alternatively you can hire canal boats or vintage bikes for the day from Bollington Wharf.

THE VIEW FROM SHINING TOR

DISTANCE/TIME	6 miles (9.7km) / 3hrs 30min
ASCENT/GRADIENT	1,150ft (351m) / ▲ ▲
PATHS	Moorland tracks with paved sections, a few places may get boggy in wet conditions, no stiles
LANDSCAPE	Rough pasture, heather moorland and woodland
SUGGESTED MAP	OS Explorer OL24 Peak District – White Peak Area
START/FINISH	Grid reference: SK012748
DOG FRIENDLINESS	Keep dogs on lead (access land, livestock and ground-nesting birds)
PARKING	Errwood Hall car park
PUBLIC TOILETS	None on route
NOTES	The Goyt Valley road is closed beyond The Street car park on Sundays and bank holidays between May and September, so park at The Street and walk along the lane to the start (adds an extra half mile (0.8km) each way)

The River Goyt begins its journey on the moors of Axe Edge and Goyt Moss before flowing northwards to join the Mersey at Stockport. An old Roman, trade and salters' route later known as The Street straddled it at Goyt Bridge before climbing over the Shining Tor ridge at Pym Chair. It is likely that an alternative version over the pass climbed more directly (and therefore steeply) through Oldgate Nick, leading to the sunken track still visible there.

In 1830, Manchester industrialist Samuel Grimshawe chose this remote valley to build Errwood Hall, as a wedding present for his son. The family imported 40,000 rhododendrons and azaleas for the gardens, using their ocean yacht, the *Mariquita*. In its heyday the estate had a staff of 20, and included a coal mine, a watermill, housing for the servants and a private school.

However, even the Grimshawes couldn't resist Stockport's ever-growing need for water, and in 1938 the house was demolished for the newly built Fernilee Reservoir. The second reservoir, the Errwood, was built higher up the valley 30 years later. Little Goyt Bridge was dismantled and rebuilt upstream, and the valley was changed forever. For a while it became the destination of seemingly every Sunday car outing from Greater Manchester, until new car parks and a one-way system initiated by the National Park Authority restored relative order to this once peaceful beauty spot.

This walk takes you back to the 19th century, to the time of the Grimshawes, but first you will get an overview of the valley by climbing the grassy spur dividing the Goyt and Shooter's Clough. You will then climb on to the high panoramic viewpoint of Shining Tor, where on a very clear day you can see past Shutlingsloe's summit as far as The Wrekin in the south and across the skyscrapers of Manchester to the Lancashire hills in the north. Stride out along the paved ridgeline to Cats Tor for another great panoramic viewpoint, then descend via The Street to a wild, partially wooded combe.

Here lies the Spanish Shrine to St Joseph, built by the Grimshawes in memory of their governess, Dolores de Ybarguen (hence D de Y inscribed in the chapel). The circular, stone-built shrine offers welcome shade on a hot summer's day, but is also still used for private religious worship, with many dedications to those no longer alive on display under the colourful mosaic.

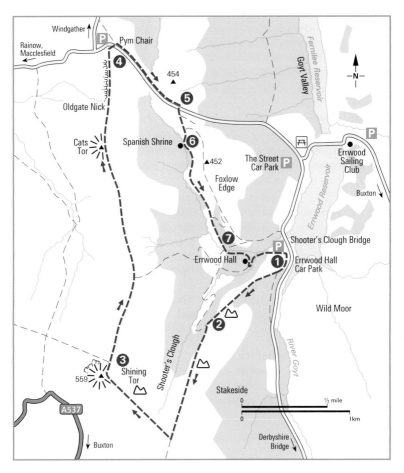

1. Just beyond the south end of the car park, take a footpath right to Stakeside. Climb through a small area of woodland then join a stone track heading uphill. Pass through a gateway and continue uphill towards Stakeside, rising up a grassy bilberry-threaded spur between sparse lines of trees.

2. Stay left of a wall on your right at a path junction, ignoring the path to Errwood Hall through the wall. Instead, take the ongoing path towards the Cat and Fiddle distillery. Shortly after a transmitter in the distance comes into view, take a footpath bearing right through a gate in the wall signed to

Shining Tor. The eroding path dips briefly then rises to the trig point on Shining Tor's summit.

3. At the summit there is a 360-degree panoramic viewpoint with views of Shutlingsloe's pointed peak, Kinder plateau, Combs Hill and Axe Edge. On exceptionally fine days you may be able to see as far as The Wrekin and beyond Manchester's skyline. A line of stone flags now leads along the broad ridgeline and across a slight saddle past Cats Tor (where the stone flags end) to Oldgate Nick (spot the holloway or sunken track) and towards Pym Chair, a legendary stone seat of a local highwayman.

4. Just before Pym Chair, cut the corner rightwards towards Windgather to avoid a short narrow and sunken section of country lane over the pass. Turn right along the lane then follow a traffic-avoiding path beside the road where a path turns left towards Windgather.

5. At an informal roadside parking area, take a footpath right towards Errwood. At the next waymarker stay right towards Errwood then take some stone steps down to the circular 'Spanish shrine' at the edge of woodland.

6. The path from the shrine continues back above the trees to rejoin the Errwood path. Descend gently above the forest on your right then more steeply down a clear tongue between woodland, passing a side path to Foxlow Edge on the way towards Errwood.

7. Turn right (again towards Errwood) at a waymarked junction, then descend a few steps towards a stream. Turn left beside the stream towards Errwood Hall – do not cross the bridge by the junction, you will cross the stream lower down on boardwalk, then rise gently on a stepped path. In early summer there is a good display of rhododendrons, then the ruins of the hall appear to your right. Descend to an oblique junction and turn left. This wide track undulates through rhododendron and oak woodland to a green forestry gate. Continue ahead and through a gap in a stone wall where the track bends right, descending grassy heathland to the car park.

Where to eat and drink

There's usually an ice-cream van in the car park at Errwood in summer. For something more substantial try The Shady Oak at Fernilee (on the A5004 between Buxton and Whaley Bridge), which serves food daily.

What to see

On the west slopes of Burbage Edge you can see the faint horizontal line of the old trackbed of the Cromford and High Peak Railway, joining a clearer holloway line which bends down towards the reservoir. Although this famous railway was one of the earliest in the country, the branch through the Goyt Valley closed in 1892.

While you're there

It is worth a wander around the various permitted paths (see map at car park) surrounding Errwood Hall to see further remnants of the once grand estate, including workers' cottages from the Castedge coal mines.

TIDESWELL AND MILLERS DALE

DISTANCE/TIME	7 miles (11.3km) / 4hrs
ASCENT/GRADIENT	1,000ft (305m) / ▲▲
PATHS	Generally well-defined paths and tracks, path at Water-cum-Jolly liable to flooding, limestone slippery and some paths muddy when wet, a few stiles towards the end
LANDSCAPE	Limestone dales, shady woodland
SUGGESTED MAP	OS Explorer OL24 Peak District – White Peak Area
START/FINISH	Grid reference: SK153741
DOG FRIENDLINESS	Dogs should be kept on lead, and should be kept out of the River Wye to protect endangered water voles
PARKING	Tideswell Dale pay car park
PUBLIC TOILETS	At car park and Tideswell village

It's all quiet in Millers Dale these days, but it wasn't always so. Many early industrialists wanted to build their cotton mills in the countryside, far away from the marauding Luddites of the city. The Wye and its tributaries had the power to work these mills. The railway followed, and that brought more industry with it. And so little Millers Dale and its neighbours joined the Industrial Revolution. The walk starts in Tideswell Dale. Nowadays it's choked with thickets and herbs but they hide a history of quarrying and mining for basalt.

Cruelty at the mill

A Memoir of Robert Blincoe, written in 1863, tells of the cruelty to child apprentices at Litton Mill. The owner, Ellis Needham, brought children from the poorhouses of London, many of whom died and were buried in the churchyards of Tideswell and Taddington. It is said that ghosts of some of the apprentices still make appearances in or around the mill. It eventually fell into a derelict state and after lying damp and neglected for many years, has now found a new lease of life as apartments.

The walk emerges from the shadows of the mill into Water-cum-Jolly. At first the river is lined by mudbanks thick with rushes and common horsetail. The river widens out and, at the same time, impressive limestone cliffs squeeze the path. The river's widening is artificial, a result of it being controlled to form a head of water for the downstream mill. Once a new hydroelectric scheme is complete it will be providing power once again. Round the next corner is Cressbrook Mill, built by Sir Richard Arkwright, but taken over by William Newton. Newton also employed child labour but was said to have treated them well. The rooftop bell tower would have peeled to beckon the apprentices, who lived next door, to the works. Like Litton, this impressive Georgian mill was allowed to moulder, but has since been restored as flats. The walk leaves the banks of the Wye at Cressbrook to take in pretty Cressbrook Dale. In this nature reserve you'll see lily of the valley, wild garlic and bloody cranesbill. Just as you think you've found your true rural retreat you'll climb to the rim of the dale, look across it and see the grassed-over spoil heaps of lead mines. Finally, the ancient strip fields of Litton form a mosaic of pasture and dry-stone walls on the return route.

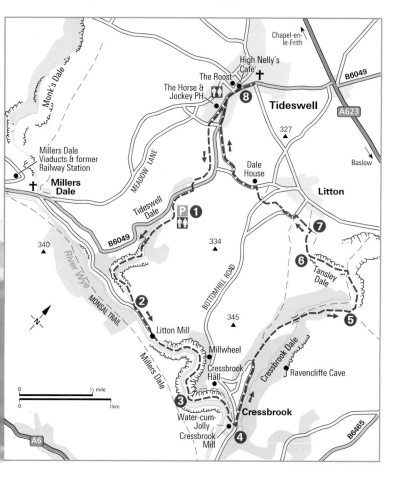

1. Follow the path southwards from beside the car park toilet block into Tideswell Dale. At a gate, stay on the main tarmac path, then fork right across a little bridge.

2. Turn left on to a tarmac road, which runs along Millers Dale to Litton Mill. A concession path leads down the mill driveway and past the mill. Swing right past the Old Gas House then left over the tail race, then follow the River Wye as it meanders through the tight, steep-sided dale.

3. The river eventually widens out at Water-cum-Jolly, the path tracing a wall of limestone cliffs. Cross the footbridge, then turn left immediately before the mill and out to the road. If flooded, a narrow signed concession path climbs steeply out before the pool then below Cressbrook Hall to the lane.

4. Turn left along the road, then fork right, climbing steadily into Cressbrook Dale. At a hairpin bend, take a track going straight ahead into the woods. Ignore a side turn left, and go through a gate into a clearing high above the stream. Follow the path downhill, forking left at the bottom to a footbridge. At a second small patch of shady woodland, fork right; this path climbs high up the valley side then emerges from the trees.

5. Fork left at a gate and down a grassy path to the dale bottom. Go right to a footbridge, cross the (often dry) stream and rise up into Tansley Dale.

6. At the head of the dale, the path curves right to climb beside a wall, then goes left through a gate. Bear right across an elongated field, then over a stile to meet a rough vehicle track, just south of Litton.

7. Fork left on this, pass a large barn, then turn left along a country lane. At the next bend left, squeeze through a stile ahead. Follow the edge of a few fields, bend left beside a fence, then right to a lane. A stile opposite marks a path going straight down the field to a lane by Dale House. Go left and then take the first right on to a narrow lane marked 'unsuitable for motors', turning right at the far end into Tideswell.

8. After looking around the village, head south down the main street, then fork right at The Horse and Jockey pub. Cross over a lane on to a stony track past workshops. Fork left at two gates in fairly quick succession; the footpath then tracks above the main road, before descending to meet it. Turn left, then take the first gate on the right across the road. Follow the path downhill back to the car park.

Where to eat and drink
Try High Nelly's Café for delicious for brunch, lunch or coffee and cake. The Roost just a few doors down, serves both hot and cold drinks and meals, snacks and takeaways. Alternatively if beer is your persuasion, The Horse and Jockey is a walker-friendly pub.

What to see
Cressbrook Dale is part of the Derbyshire Dales National Nature Reserve. On the limestone grassland you may see orchids, cranesbill, mountain pansy, globeflower and spring sandwort. One of the many limestone-loving plants is the Nottingham catchfly, which loves dry, stony places. The white flowers roll back in daytime but are fragrant at night. In Tideswell an innovative use of a former phone box dials up audio of historic experiences.

While you're there
Visit the Millers Dale viaducts and old railway station. Built in 1863 for the Midland Railway, the site was once the Midland Line's largest railway station complete with its own post office on the platforms. The line closed in 1967 and wild flowers now line the sides of the trackbed.

LINACRE'S WOOD AND RESERVOIR

DISTANCE/TIME	5.5 miles (8.9km) / 3hrs
ASCENT/GRADIENT	785ft (239m) / ▲
PATHS	Generally good paths and tracks, field and woodland paths can be muddy at times of high rainfall, a couple of sections of pavement
LANDSCAPE	Wooded valley and pastured hillsides
SUGGESTED MAP	OS Explorer OL24 Peak District – White Peak Area
START/FINISH	Grid reference: SK336727
DOG FRIENDLINESS	Keep dogs on lead in Linacre and farmland; under close control everywhere else
PARKING	Linacre Wood car park, reached from B6050 west of Cutthorpe
PUBLIC TOILETS	Southeast of car park by Ranger's Office

It's easy to forget, as you look across Linacre and the valley of Holme Brook today, that Chesterfield is only a few miles away. This tranquil combe is sheltered from the west winds by the high Pennine heather moors. Three reservoirs are surrounded by attractive woodland. Linacre means arable land where flax is grown and, as early as the 13th century, linen from that flax was manufactured in the valley. But until the mid-19th century this was no more than an agricultural backwater of northeast Derbyshire.

Good supply

It was the growth of Chesterfield and the Derbyshire coalfields, and the need for water, that brought the valley to notice. Here was a good supply, well fed by those moors to the east. The reservoirs were built one by one between 1855 and 1904 in an attempt to supply these ever-growing requirements. Until 1909, when they built the filter beds, water was pumped direct from the reservoirs to consumers' homes. According to the information sign at Linacre Reservoir the 'water supply was such that the poor used it as soup, the middle class for washing their clothes and the elite for watering their gardens'.

If you've parked in the middle car park, you're standing above the ruins of two great buildings. Not much is known about the older Linacre Hall other than its mention in old charters, but the three-storey mansion of Linacre House was once home to Dr Thomas Linacre (1460–1524), who was president of the Royal College of Surgeons and physician to both Henry VIII and the young Mary, Queen of Scots.

Some steps take you down to the dam of the middle reservoir, and through peaceful Linacre Wood. Although many conifers have been planted for the protection of the reservoirs, about two-thirds of the trees are broad-leaved, mainly sycamore, beech, oak and ash. The remaining third are larch, pine and spruce. Hidden in the woods you may discover the remains of some old Q-holes. These were crudely dug pits of about 5ft (1.5m) diameter where timber was once burnt for use in the smelting of lead ore. This was a widespread practice in the 17th century.

Beyond the reservoirs the route climbs out through a wooded clough, passing the hillside hamlet of Wigley before descending into the next valley by the ancient track of Bagthorpe Lane. Frith Hall near the valley bottom has a large medieval cruck-framed barn. The route climbs back out of the valley to Old Brampton. This straggling village is dominated by the broad-spired tower of the 14th-century parish church of St Peter and St Paul. The oak doors came from the chapel of Derwent Hall before it was submerged beneath Ladybower Reservoir. Take a look at the clock. Can you notice the mistake? It has 63 minutes painted on its face. That gives you a bit more time to stroll down a walled lane to get back to Linacre Wood.

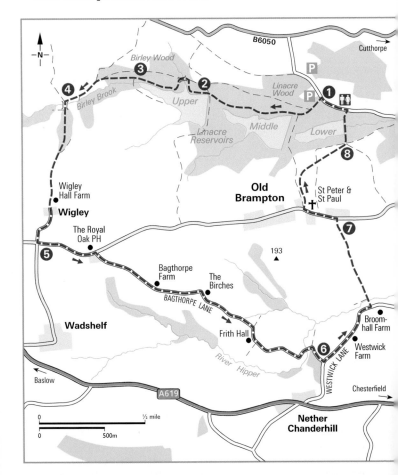

1. From the information board in the lower car park, take a path that descends into the woods. At the bottom, go right on a broad bridleway. Approaching the dam of the middle reservoir, keep right to pass a small picnic area and wind on above the lake.

2. Several paths converge near the top dam; continue slightly right then ahead on a broad track through the trees above the shore. At a side stream cross the lower of the two bridges and carry on to the head of the reservoir.

3. Ignore the bridge over Birley Brook and instead follow the stream up the narrowing valley. Towards the edge of woodland, take the upper of two gates (the one marked as a public footpath) into scrubby woodland below a field. Descend through scrub on to a small grassy meadow. Stepping stones take the path over a side stream into another broad grassy swathe footing a slope.

4. Disregard a footbridge on the left but soon after take another bridge across the brook, then climb a stile and cross a slab bridge in quick succession. The path fords another stream then winds it way up through the trees. Leaving the trees, walk past a barn behind Wigley Hall Farm and keep going to join a lane. Follow this out to the main road.

5. Cross the road and go left towards Old Brampton. Just beyond The Royal Oak turn right down an initially metalled bridleway, Bagthorpe Lane, following it past a farm (Bagthorpe). Swing right before the gates of a large farm and stables (The Birches). Continue down into the valley of the River Hipper, passing through a farmyard either side of the river and climbing to a country lane.

6. Turn left along this, descending past Westwick Farm. Bend sharp right then fork left just before another farm (Broomhall). Cross the river then continue straight ahead up the other side of the valley into Old Brampton.

7. Turn left along the lane, passing 'the church with extra minutes on its clock'. At the far end of the village, turn right by Hill Crest on to a bridleway track. Fork right and diagonally across an arable field as the track bends right and into trees.

8. Re-enter woodland through a wall gap. At a junction of paths turn left through the gate before descending to the dam. Beyond, walk up a stepped path. Fork right opposite a gate to reach the main park drive by the Ranger's Office. Go left, on the main tarmac driveway back to the car park.

Where to eat and drink
The Royal Oak near Wigley (closed Monday and Tuesday) is passed halfway round the walk, while The Three Merry Lads serves appetising food and is just a short drive to the east along the B6050 in Cutthorpe.

What to see
In spring, the woodland floor is covered with bluebells and wild garlic. On the water you'll probably see moorhens and mallards and maybe some of the migrating wildfowl that frequently visit.

While you're there
Chesterfield is well worth a visit. It's a historic town dating back to Roman times. The parish church has a curious crooked spire. One of the more credible theories for the leaning is that the Black Death killed off many of the craftsmen of the time, and those left used unseasoned timber that buckled with the weight of the leading.

CHATSWORTH PARK AND GARDENS

DISTANCE/TIME	5.4 miles (8.7km) / 3hrs
ASCENT/GRADIENT	655ft (200m) / ▲
PATHS	Mostly good paths and forest trails, estate roads, rougher and sometimes muddy in deer park, narrow road bridge, no pavement at Calton Lees Bridge, 2 stiles
LANDSCAPE	Parkland, woodland and rugged moorland
SUGGESTED MAP	OS Explorer OL24 Peak District – White Peak Area
START/FINISH	Grid reference: SK261703
DOG FRIENDLINESS	Keep on lead at all times
PARKING	Chatsworth House car park (pay car park)
PUBLIC TOILETS	In the stable block
NOTES	Many of the paths are permissive and may be closed occasionally when special events are running. Check the Chatsworth House website for details

Sitting on the banks of the River Derwent, surrounded by lush green parkland, moors and a backdrop of wooded hillsides, Chatsworth is one of the most elegant and popular of England's stately homes. First opened to the public in 1844 it continues to attract large numbers of visitors.

Work first started on the house in 1549 when Sir William Cavendish acquired the land and set about building a mansion. He died before it was completed and it was finished by his widow, Bess of Hardwick, who by the simple expedient of marrying four times, each time to a more powerful and richer man, succeeded in becoming the richest woman in England after the queen. Bess left Chatsworth to her son Henry Cavendish, who sold it to his brother William, the 1st Earl of Devonshire. It has now been home to 14 generations of the Cavendish family and is the seat of the current Duke and Duchess of Devonshire.

Initially a three-storey Elizabethan mansion, the house has been significantly altered and added to over the centuries. The 4th Earl, who was later made 1st Duke of Devonshire for his support of William III in the 'Glorious Revolution' of 1688, practically rebuilt it. Towards the end of the 18th century the 4th Duke had the magnificent baroque stables built and engaged the services of the famous landscape gardener Lancelot 'Capability' Brown, and it is the gardens and parkland (covering 1,000 acres (405ha)) that draw visitors back again and again. There are rare trees, sculptures, fountains and gardens, as well as a maze and adventure playground. The Emperor Fountain in the long canal pond, built in 1844 by Chatsworth's head gardener, Joseph Paxton, is the highest gravity-fed fountain in the world. Paxton also built a great conservatory at Chatsworth and went on to design the Crystal Palace for the Great Exhibition in London in 1851. Knighted by Queen Victoria, he later became a Member of Parliament and is buried in the churchyard at Edensor.

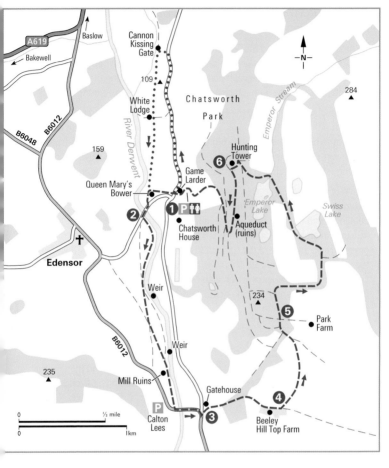

1. Head to the bottom of the car park, and pass the former Game Larder. Now follow exit signs out to the northern edge of the car park. Take the pedestrian/'estate traffic only' tarmac track heading north. For the walk extension continue ahead, otherwise cut across parkland left towards Queen Mary's Bower. Head left and back through a gate to the main drive to Chatsworth House then cross the road bridge on your right.

2. Immediately after the bridge, cross the road and walk downhill to the riverbank. Follow the River Derwent past a couple of weirs and the remains of an old mill to the next bridge which carries the B6012 over the river. Go through a metal kissing gate on to the road and across the narrow bridge.

3. At the bend in the road, take the second of two tarmac tracks on the bend and to the right of a gatehouse to the estate. Continue uphill, past Beeley Hill Top Farm.

4. Immediately after the farm, cross a stile on the left, taking a concession path across the field. Go through an ordinary gate then a deer fence gate, then bend left on a well-defined path through bracken. This crosses occasional board-walks and narrows somewhat as it rises. Go through another deer fence, then turn left on to a broad track. Cross the wall into the estate by a high stile and continue to a crossroads.

5. Go straight ahead and follow the track as it passes the Swiss Lake on the right and then loops round Emperor Lake on the left. When you reach a junction of tracks by a telegraph pole, continue briefly along the main track to reach a crossroads with a tarmac lane. Turn left for the Hunting Tower.

6. Descend steps in front of the Hunting Tower to return to the tarmac track. Turn left along this. It now takes a long lazy zigzag downhill, passing what appears to be the remains of an old aqueduct (with water cascading from the end in wet conditions), then doubling back. Continue downhill, eventually turning left by the farmyard entrance and down to the car park at Chatsworth House.

Extending the walk Follow the pedestrian/'estate traffic only' tarmac track heading north until you are within sight of the gates at the end of the estate. At a grey metal roadside box, turn left across the park on a wide but faint grassy track. Just before the Cannon Kissing Gate (which leads to Baslow) turn left on to a gravel trail. This runs along the edge of the estate past White Lodge (a private residence which also contains Paxton's former dwelling – Barbrook House) and the cricket club. Continue past Queen Mary's Bower to return to the main route.

Where to eat and drink
Most of the free-to-enter dining options can be found around the courtyard of James Paine's 18th-century stable buildings. Cavendish Restaurant is the formal option; while the Carriage House offers excellent meals in a self-service, fully licensed restaurant. Afternoon teas are available in the Flying Childers Bar. There's also a Gin Bar and ice-cream kiosk in the courtyard. The Food To Go outlet offers snacks.

What to see
The Game Larder at the bottom of the main car park was restored in 2016 and offers interesting visitor information. Legend has it that the nearby Queen Mary's Bower was built to provide a raised exercise area for Mary, Queen of Scots while she was held captive in Chatsworth in the 1570s. However, current thinking is that its original purpose was as a garden feature when the land around once contained ponds.

While you're there
Visit Edensor village, whose houses are all individually styled. The Cavendish burial plot can be found at the top of the church's graveyard, where Kathleen Kennedy, sister of John F Kennedy, is buried. Kathleen became the wife of the 10th Duke's eldest son in 1944, four months before he was killed in World War II.

26

ASHFORD-IN-THE-WATER AND MONSAL DALE

DISTANCE/TIME	6 miles (9.7km) / 3hrs 30min
ASCENT/GRADIENT	1,100ft (335m) / ▲ ▲
PATHS	Well-defined paths and tracks throughout, a few short rougher sections in Deep Dale and Great Shacklow Wood, a few stiles
LANDSCAPE	Limestone dales and high pasture
SUGGESTED MAP	OS Explorer OL24 Peak District – White Peak Area
START/FINISH	Grid reference: SK194697
DOG FRIENDLINESS	Under close control and on lead near livestock
PARKING	Ashford-in-the-Water pay car park
PUBLIC TOILETS	At Ashford car park, White Lodge and Monsal Head
NOTES	Waymarked path follows a very short section of rough and mossy limestone valley base near Deep Dale. In unusually wet conditions this may be rather wet and slippery underfoot

The Wye is a chameleon among rivers. Rising as a peaty stream from Axe Edge, it rushes downhill, only to be confined by the concrete and tarmac of Buxton, a spa town, and the quarries to the east. Beyond Chee Dale it gets renewed vigour and cuts a deep gorge through beds of limestone, finally to calm down again among the gentle landscape of Bakewell. The finest stretch of the river valley must be around Monsal Head, and the best approach is that from Ashford-in-the-Water, one of Derbyshire's prettiest villages.

Leaving Ashford's streets behind, the route climbs to high pastures that give no clue as to the whereabouts of Monsal Dale. But suddenly you reach the last wall and the ground falls away into a deep wooded gorge. John Ruskin was so taken with this beauty that he likened it to the Vale of Tempe: 'you might have seen the Gods there morning and evening – Apollo and all the sweet Muses of the light – walking in fair procession on the lawns of it, and to and fro among the pinnacles of its crags.'

It's just a short walk along the rim to reach one of Derbyshire's best-known viewpoints, where the Monsal Viaduct spans the gorge. Built in 1867 as part of the Midland Railway's line to Buxton, the five-arched, stone-built viaduct is nearly 80ft (26m) high. The building of this angered Ruskin. He continued: 'you blasted its rocks away, heaped thousands of tons of shale into its lovely stream. The valley is gone, and the Gods with it.' The line closed in 1968 and the rails were ripped out, leaving only the trackbed and the bridges. Ironically, today's conservationists have placed a conservation order on the viaduct. The trackbed is used as a recreational route for walkers and cyclists: the Monsal Trail. The walk continues over the viaduct, giving bird's-eye views of the river and the lawn-like surrounding pastures. It then descends to the riverbank, following it westwards under the viaduct and beneath the peak of Fin Cop. The valley curves like a sickle, while the path weaves in and out of thickets and by wetlands. After crossing the A6 the route takes you into the mouth of Deep Dale, then the shade of Great Shacklow Wood. Just past some pools filled with trout there's an entrance to the Magpie Mine Sough. The tunnel was built in 1873 to drain the Magpie Lead Mines at nearby Sheldon.

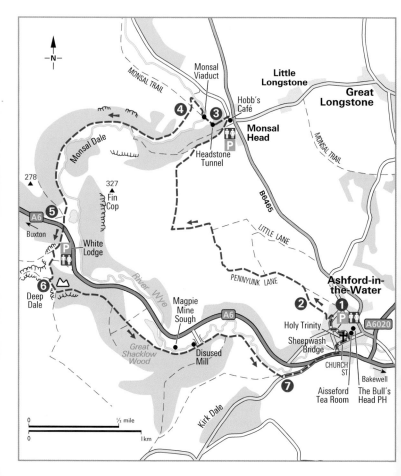

1. From the car park, leave Corner Cottage on your left then turn right along Vicarage Lane. By a yellow grit bin, a footpath doubles back left, then swings sharp right to climb behind housing. Beyond a narrow gate the path enters a field.

2. Head uphill, curving to a stile in the distant right corner that leads on to a walled stony track (Pennyunk Lane) which winds among high pastures. At the end, go left uphill along a field edge. Go through a gate at the top, turn right past a dew pond and carry on as the track resumes. Emerging above the rim of Monsal Dale, fork right along a path to the car park at Monsal Head.

3. After admiring the view, take the continuing path signed 'Monsal Trail and Viaduct', descending steeply on steps. Fork left at a junction towards 'Viaduct and Monsal Trail', descending to the trail at the western portal of the Headstone Tunnel. Cross the viaduct, then fork right through a gate towards 'Monsal Head via Netherdale' at a junction of bridleways. Turn right along the valley, go underneath the viaduct and through a squeeze stile.

4. The onward path heads downriver, more or less beside the Wye. Eventually, at a path junction, continue towards 'A6 and White Lodge', crossing a stream and stile, then up to the A6.

5. Cross this busy road and enter the White Lodge car park. By the pay station, take a path signed 'Deep Dale Nature Reserve Ashford'. Beyond a gate, ignore a path to Taddington. Bend right on worn limestone pavement, and go briefly up a mossy rough limestone section beside a wall to cross a stile into the Deep Dale Nature Reserve. Rise up a rough track, then fork left at a junction towards Ashford and Sheldon rising steeply to a junction at the edge of woodland.

6. Go through the gate towards Ashford, continuing more easily across then gently descending the steep slopes of Great Shacklow Wood. Disregard a later crossing path from Sheldon, but then watch for the drain outflow from the Magpie Mine. Beyond a derelict bone mill, leave the wood and carry on ahead along a broader track, shortly passing the foot of a side dale. Bend left through a gate, then follow the river, ultimately passing through two gates to meet a lane at the bottom of Kirk Dale.

7. Turn left down to the A6 and then right along the pavement towards Ashford. Cross the busy road then fork left over Sheepwash Bridge. Continue up Fennel Street then right to return to the car park.

Where to eat and drink
In Ashford, The Bull's Head is popular for real ale and pub meals. Aisseford Tea Room in Ashford and Hobb's Café at Monsal Head (open Friday–Sunday 10am–3pm) are ideal for hot drinks and cakes.

What to see
The fabulous and much-photographed view of (and from) the Monsal Viaduct. Ashford's 17th-century Sheepwash Bridge over the River Wye was built on the original site of the ford that gave the village its name. On the far side of the bridge is where the sheep were gathered for washing.

While you're there
Bakewell, next door to Ashford, is well worth a visit. This bustling town is built round a fine 14th-century bridge over the River Wye. Buxton is somewhat further away, but its Museum and Art Gallery holds a large collection of Ashford marble, which can also be seen in the chapel at Chatsworth House. The rock is an impure local limestone infused with natural bitumen, which becomes shiny and jet black when polished. The majority of this 'marble' came from two local quarries in the 18th and 19th centuries, and it has been highly prized by dignities including Bess of Hardwick and Queen Victoria.

CHROME HILL FROM EARL STERNDALE

DISTANCE/TIME	6.3 miles (10.3km) / 4hrs
ASCENT/GRADIENT	1,280ft (390m) / ▲ ▲ ▲
PATHS	Mostly reasonable paths and tracks, but some are rugged, steep ridgeline, can be muddy or slippery after rain
LANDSCAPE	Gritstone moors and cloughs with limestone hills
SUGGESTED MAP	OS Explorer OL24 Peak District – White Peak Area
START/FINISH	Grid reference: SK090670
DOG FRIENDLINESS	Farmland; dogs should be kept under close control
PARKING	On roadside in Earl Sterndale (limited space)
PUBLIC TOILETS	None on route

At the far end of the Dove Valley stands Axe Edge. This is the Pennine watershed and near to here five rivers – the Goyt, the Dane, the Dove, the Wye and the Manifold – go their separate ways towards the Irish and North Seas. You're 1,660ft (506m) above sea level on one of the wildest gritstone moors of the Dark Peak, but when you look east you're looking across to the White Peak valley of the Dove. It's a fascinating view with several rocky hills vying for attention. One angular hill stands out from all the rest that's Chrome Hill, and it's the highpoint of the day. It's tough and rugged going from that direction though, so this walk starts more gently from Earl Sterndale to the southeast. There's a fabulous view over Parkhouse and Chrome Hills from Hitter Hill, but the direct descent is steep, so a less steep way snakes diagonally down to the valley, then below Parkhouse Hill.

The Dragon's Back

Chrome Hill and its neighbours are the remains of coral reefs formed over 320 million years ago, when Derbyshire lay under a warm tropical sea near the equator. Arches and caves, spires and fissures have been carved out of the coral and you can see why it's sometimes known as the Dragon's Back. There's a steep downhill section to do before the climb, then the footpath seems to take a timid line along the west side. Just as you think you've missed the summit path, the one you're on turns left and climbs for the sky. The path doesn't always keep to the crest, but avoids mild scrambles by plotting a devious course round the top rocks. Experienced walkers with a head for heights may well prefer to 'ride the dragon's back'. From the top, Parkhouse Hill captures your attention. It's not unlike Chrome Hill, but the start and ridgeline is very tough with some awkward discontinuous sections where the ridge drops down a crag. If you've found Chrome Hill easy then give it a go. This route descends to the little road at its foot, and takes a good look from below before following a path across the pastures to its west.

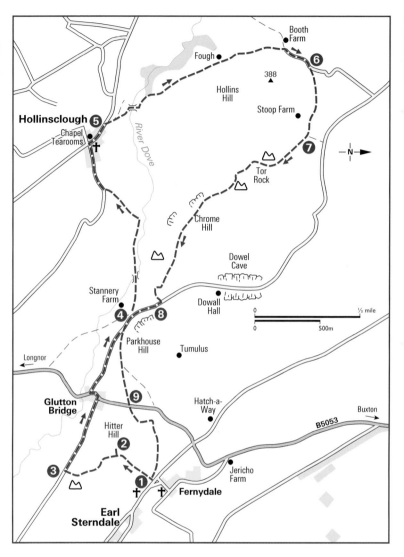

1. From the green in the centre of the village, skirt to the right of a pub (currently closed), then bend left around it, following footpath waymarkers towards Longnor as the path divides. Go through a gate with a yellow-topped post and rise gently up through fields. Cross a rough stile on to the higher ground of Hitter Hill. The summit is unmarked but in line with the ridge from Parkhouse and Chrome to the north.

2. The descent to the far corner of access land is very steep, so return to the previous stile then head right along the field edge-top, to a stile in the corner. Continue briefly along the top edge in the next field, then fork right at a waymarker to Longnor. This narrow path descends diagonally across fields on a steep hillside to a tarmac track by a farm.

3. Fork right along this track. At Glutton Bridge, turn left along a road, then next right up a narrow lane. This leads underneath the western flanks of Parkhouse Hill.

4. As the road bends right to cross the col between Parkhouse and Chrome Hills, fork left on to a byway, which initially runs along Stannery Farm's driveway. Follow signs to Hollinsclough, ignore a left fork, then bypass a ford on a footbridge. At a T-junction of farm tracks go left. At a surfaced lane, go right then right again in Hollinsclough.

5. At the edge of the village, fork right through a gate on to a footpath. Bend right and down to cross an old stone footbridge. Go through an old metal gate and bend left up a bridleway track. At the top, turn left on to a farm track. Follow this all the way to a junction with a tarmac lane near Booth Farm and turn right.

6. At a bend left, fork right over a stile on a concession path which follows a farm track to a pair of gates. Cross a stile by the left gate then follow way-marker posts gently left to a wall stile. Bend slightly left at a gate, reaching a track by a waymarked junction. Continue towards Chrome Hill with the top wall on your left.

7. Go through three gates, then follow waymarkers near a field edge and steeply downhill. Cross a gate on your left; at the next gate, climb left to the ridge. Turn right along the ridge to follow the path over Chrome Hill, bending left at the end to the lane beneath Parkhouse Hill.

8. Head southwards down the lane, forking left on to a footpath that veers gently away from the road under the western slopes of Parkhouse Hill.

9. Cross the road and back into fields, heading diagonally left across rough trackless ground. Head directly across the next field, then diagonally right across a third, passing a jutting-out wall corner on your left. Pass through four gates in quick succession near a house to return to the green.

Where to eat and drink

The Chapel Tea Rooms in Hollinsclough serves hot drinks, light bites and cake. It's opposite the Methodist Church, open weekends only. The Pack Horse Inn in Crowdecote serves good meals made with locally sourced ingredients and local ales. Closed on Mondays and Tuesdays.

What to see

The elements have carved out arches and caves in the Carboniferous limestone, making Chrome Hill a fascinating place for geologists. You may spot fossils in the stones of the limestone walls. Limestone-loving plants such as field scabious and harebells can be seen.

While you're there

Pilsbury Castle is some distance to the south of Crowdecote, further down the Dove Valley. Its ruined earthworks are all that remains of the once imposing castle that controlled this part of the Dove Valley, but it's impressive all the same.

SHUTLINGSLOE AND THE MACCLESFIELD FOREST

DISTANCE/TIME	6.7 miles (10.8km) / 4hrs
ASCENT/GRADIENT	1,270ft (387m) / ▲ ▲
PATHS	Sloping field paths, lanes and easy forest tracks, steep hillside, many stiles
LANDSCAPE	Rough pasture, angular hills, plus large tracts of woodland
SUGGESTED MAP	OS Explorer OL24 Peak District – White Peak Area
START/FINISH	Grid reference: SJ982681
DOG FRIENDLINESS	Dogs should be kept under close control and on lead across the moor. Cows with calves may be present below Higher Nabbs farm; if present, follow directions at field entrance
PARKING	Lay-by at Brookside, on lane 0.25 miles (400m) south of The Crag Inn
PUBLIC TOILETS	At Forest Ranger Centre

The Royal Forest of Macclesfield was once the preserve of the nobility, an extensive hunting ground for the royal court searching for deer and boar. It covered a large area, stretching across from the Cheshire Plain to the valleys of the Goyt and Dane, but most of the so-called 'forest' was probably little more than open ground or scrub, with large tracts of high and inhospitable moorland. In the 1400s Henry VI appointed John Stanley as Steward of Macclesfield Forest, and it was his son Thomas (later Baron Stanley) who played a crucial role in the Battle of Bosworth in 1485 to ensure the victory of his stepson the Earl of Richmond, who became Henry VII. The grateful new king made Stanley the Earl of Derby, and the office of Steward of Macclesfield Forest became a hereditary position.

The Forest Laws that operated in the hunting lands until Elizabethan times were extremely strict. There were severe penalties for anyone caught poaching, as testified by the name of the isolated hilltop pub, the Hanging Gate, that the walk visits at Higher Sutton. Near the start of the walk is the equally descriptive Crag Inn, tucked away above Clough Brook at Wildboarclough. But whether, according to local tradition, 'the ravine of the wild boar' is indeed the location of the last of its kind killed in England during the 15th century is open to doubt. Looming above Wildboarclough is the coned peak of Shutlingsloe, which at 1,659ft (506m) offers a full 360-degree panoramic view over Cheshire, Staffordshire and Derbyshire.

Later on is Tegg's Nose, a gritstone outcrop to the north that protrudes above the dark-green conifers of the present-day Macclesfield Forest. This modern plantation produces timber rather than venison and provides encouragement for wildlife. Walkers are welcome to explore the forest's many paths and tracks. Look out for the occasional wooden sculpture, and wildlife such as crossbills and woodpeckers, stoats and foxes. The heronry in the larch trees on the eastern shore of Trentabank Reservoir is the largest in the Peak District. In addition, the forest is home to red deer.

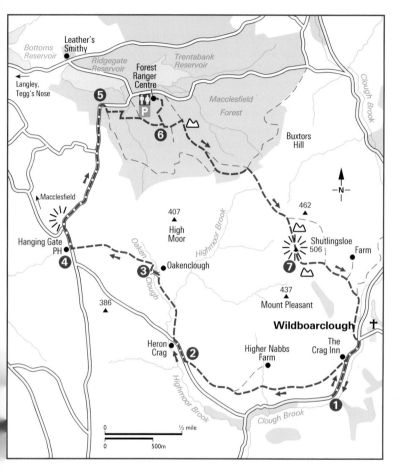

1. Walk up the road to The Crag Inn. Go through a gate beside the car park entrance and double back left on a grass pathway above the lane. Guiding way-markers indicate the route across the hillside, gently gaining height over successive fields. Detour briefly to the right to cross a stream below Higher Nabbs Farm, then return to your original course, rising gently to a wall stile which leads out on to a metalled track. Follow this downhill to a junction.

2. Turn right and walk along the lane past Heron Crag to a bridge. Go through a kissing gate on the right and follow the path near the stream. After a gate, cross a bridge. The path now twists across a stream then follows its valley (Oaken Clough) uphill, passing through another gate just below some power lines. Towards the top, turn left and cross the stream on a permissive path just below a house, following waymarkers past a pond to a driveway. Turn left through a gate and climb beside a wall.

3. A gate at the top leads across moorland on a grassy track, which can be boggy when wet. Later join a wall on the right, then swing right through a gateway and then go left over a stile. Follow a sunken track down to emerge opposite the Hanging Gate pub.

4. Turn right on to the tarmac lane, then fork right at a hairpin bend. Keep straight on past a side road then bend right into Macclesfield Forest.

5. Turn right through a wide forestry gateway. Ignore the broad track signed 'Shutlingsloe' and instead take a footpath left and parallel with the road towards Trentabank. A zigzag descent leads to a junction of paths with a red-banded waymarker. Cross a broad track then turn right at another red waymarker to wind your way up through the forest to reach another junction.

6. The Forest Ranger Centre is a short detour to the left, but Shutlingsloe lies to the right. Rise to a broader track and go left. At a junction by a gate, turn right and climb steadily through the forest, passing a barrier at the top. Join a forest bridleway which rounds a bowl of recently cleared plantation, then just after a vehicle turning area, fork right up a track towards Shutlingsloe. Pass through a gate and follow a slabbed path across the moor towards Wildboarclough. Shutlingsloe's iconic conical summit soon comes into view. Go through a gate, turn right and continue by the wall line. A steepening and surprisingly strenuous slabbed path leads to the top.

7. From the summit head briefly south, then descend an eroded path down the steep eastern slope of the hill, to an open farm drive. Turn right on to this, then follow it all the way down to the road and turn right to return to the car park.

Where to eat and drink

The Crag Inn at Wildboarclough has a lovely outdoors seating area and serves good food. Check their website for current opening hours. The Leathers Smithy near Trentabank is also worth a visit. At weekends, The Forest Snug snack van is often found by the Macclesfield Forest Ranger Centre.

What to see

At first glance Wildboarclough might seem a sleepy and uneventful place, but in fact it was once a hive of industrial activity. Two centuries ago Clough Brook was harnessed to provide power for local textile mills, and a calico-printing factory known as Crag Works was established. Stanley Pool, visible from the summit of Shutlingsloe towards the church, was constructed to power the works, but nothing remains of its 30ft (9m) water wheel. These days the nearest industry is Forest Distillers who produce artisanal gin a few miles up the road.

While you're there

If the scramble up to the summit has whetted your appetite for climbing, then the bouldering wall at the Macclesfield Activity Centre might be of interest. For something more sedate, try Lyme Park in nearby Disley for its grand stately mansion.

THE ROACHES AND LUD'S CHURCH

DISTANCE/TIME	5.3 miles (8.4km) / 3hrs
ASCENT/GRADIENT	790ft (241m) / ▲▲▲
PATHS	Rocky moorland paths, forest tracks, occasionally boggy, quiet road
LANDSCAPE	Moor and woodland
SUGGESTED MAP	OS Explorer OL24 Peak District – White Peak Area
START/FINISH	Grid reference: SJ999662
DOG FRIENDLINESS	Keep on lead on access land
PARKING	Gradbach Staffordshire Wildlife Trust car park (donation requested)
PUBLIC TOILETS	None on route

The jagged ridge of The Roaches is one of the most popular locations in the Peak District National Park, a magnet for walkers and climbers with good paths, challenging climbs and terrific views from the top. This walk explores a quieter ridge off the northern end, but the panorama is no less splendid. To the south, below The Roaches, is Tittesworth Reservoir and distant Leek; over to the west is the distinctive jutting outline of The Cloud, near Congleton; while northwards is the equally unmistakable pointed summit of Shutlingsloe. You start, however, along a quiet lane to the dark and mysterious woodland of the Dane Valley passing the former silk-spinning Gradbach Mill on the way. Crossing the River Dane, it's then a steep pull up through the forest to gain the spectacular views from the moorland ridgeline. But the most unexpected view is deep in the forest.

The Green Knight

Lud's Church is a small chasm in the rocks, caused long ago by a landslip. It's a dark and atmospheric place, reputedly used as a hideaway and even a place of worship over the years, and inevitably associated with myth and legend – and they don't come much better than King Arthur. According to the 14th-century poem *Sir Gawain and the Green Knight*, a knight on horseback, clothed entirely in green, gatecrashed a feast at Camelot and challenged the Knights of the Round Table. Sir Gawain rose to the challenge and beheaded the Green Knight, but the latter retrieved his head and laughingly challenged Sir Gawain to meet with him again, in a year's time, at the Green Chapel.

In 1958 Professor Ralph Elliott identified The Roaches as the general location of the chapel from the text: 'Great crooked crags, cruelly jagged, the bristling barbs of rock seemed to brush the sky.' Professor Elliott's theory was supported by a group of linguists, working on the poem at the same time, who placed the work in the same 15-mile (24km) radius. The professor and a group of students from Keele University searched the countryside looking for a suitable cave to match the description, and Lud's Church fitted the bill.

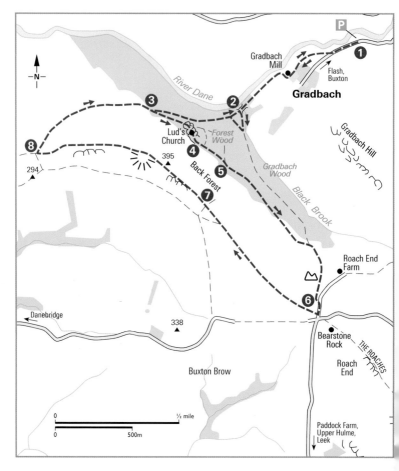

1. From the car park head right on the lane, rising up the hill then forking right down Gradbach Mill's driveway. At the mill, take a footpath directly opposite the main mill building, bending left and above the mill café. The path descends by a fence then squeezes right through a stile before maintaining its direction on the far side of a wall. This broadens into an access track. At a hairpin bend, leave the track via a wall stile directly ahead.

2. Turn right on to a path and down to cross a footbridge over the Black Brook. Fork left along the riverbank towards The Roaches. Take the next fork right towards Lud's Church on a long incline across the woods. Ignore the junction above the footbridge then rise up to a junction by a rocky outcrop.

3. Turn left here towards Lud's Church. Just beyond some wooden railings at a widening of the path, look for a small sign carved in a rock. This marks the entrance to Lud's Church.

4. Explore Lud's Church, then go up some steps at the far end of the deep chasm. Bend left to a junction by some wooden railings, then continue ahead and over sections of boardwalk. Descend to a junction with a ridge access path,

then contour along towards Gradbach and The Roaches descending shortly to another junction where you fork right towards The Roaches.

5. The path follows near the top of woodland then drops to meet a path on a stand of beech trees on a slight ridge. Fork right here, continuing towards The Roaches. Cross a small brook then continue up the paved path. As you exit woodland, keep the wall on your left-hand side, rising to the road at Roach End.

6. Just before the road, fork right and through a gate on to a wide track alongside a wall on the left. Ignore a fork left, instead continuing along the ridgeline concessionary path marked 'Swythamley via Ridge'.

7. Continue straight ahead at a crossroads in a slight dip (towards Swythamley and Danebridge). Cross through a gate in the wall and continue beside a wall on to an outcrop. The ridgeline path now undulates over a couple of dips then drops over slightly rockier ground to a path junction by a large gate.

8. Turn right on to the bridleway signed 'Gradbach and Lud's Church'. This can be popular with mountain bikers but is a lovely holloway (a sunken path trodden over centuries). This passes a rocky outcrop on your left where you rejoin your outward path. Towards the bottom of the long incline, fork left to shortcut directly down to the River Dane, crossing over two junctions. Now retrace your outward steps back to the car park.

Where to eat and drink

Gradbach Mill has an outdoor café offering light snacks, drinks and ice creams in a pretty courtyard by the river. The menu changes frequently, but the scones with real clotted cream or artisan sandwiches are often popular favourites, open from Easter to October. Alternatively try The Roaches Tea Rooms at Upper Hulme, which is open all year and sits beneath the huge rocky outcrop of Hen Cloud. The food is home-made, excellent, and there's plenty of it.

What to see

Strange but true, the Staffordshire Moorlands was once famous for its wallabies. Five escaped from a private zoo at Swythamley in 1939 and, surviving on a diet of moorland vegetation, they prospered so much that by the 1960s their colony had grown to over 50. After that they declined and it was thought they had disappeared altogether by the 1990s, but they are secretive and nocturnal animals so no one is absolutely sure, although sadly the 2018 moorland fire may have been the last straw for them.

While you're there

Just a short distance north, the River Dane meets three counties bordering each other at Three Shires Heads. The Panniers Pool is a popular beauty spot and can be surprisingly busy on a hot summer's day with children paddling in the spot where packhorses would once have stopped for a rest and a drink of cooling water.

FLASH – THE HIGHEST VILLAGE

DISTANCE/TIME	5.9 miles (9.5km) / 3hrs 30min
ASCENT/GRADIENT	1,080ft (330m) / ▲ ▲
PATHS	Field and rugged moorland paths, can be boggy after rain, some roads, many stiles
LANDSCAPE	Hills, moorland and meadows
SUGGESTED MAP	OS Explorer OL24 Peak District – White Peak Area
START/FINISH	Grid reference: SK026672
DOG FRIENDLINESS	Keep on lead near livestock, cattle may be present
PARKING	Small car park on Brown Lane, near church
PUBLIC TOILETS	None on route

At an altitude of 1,518ft (463m), Flash proclaims itself the 'Highest Village in Britain'. At this elevation, winters come early and linger long. They can be cold too. Once, during wartime, it got so cold that the vicar had icicles on his ears when he reached the church.

Despite being a devout community, Flash also has the dubious honour of giving its name to sharp practice. The terms 'flash money' and 'flash company' also entered the English language as a consequence of events in Flash. A group of peddlers living near the village travelled the country hawking ribbons, buttons and goods. Known as 'Flash men' they initially paid for their goods with hard cash but, after establishing credit, they vanished with the goods and moved on to another supplier. Their name became associated with ne'er-do-wells in taverns, who helped people drink their money and were never seen again, as typified in the 18th-century folk-song, 'Flash Company':

Fiddling and dancing were all my delight
But keeping flash company has ruined me quite

'Flash money', on the other hand, referred to counterfeit bank notes, manufactured in the 18th century by a devious local gang using button presses. They were captured when a servant girl exposed them to the authorities. Some of the gang members were hanged at Chester. Flash was the ideal location for avoiding the law because of its proximity to the borders of three counties; police in one county could not pursue miscreants into another.

A local beauty spot called Three Shires Heads, about a mile (1.6km) northwest of the village, by a packhorse bridge, is the meeting place of Derbyshire, Cheshire and Staffordshire. Illegal bare-knuckle fights were held here and, when the police arrived, the participants simply crossed the bridge and continued their bout on the other side. More peaceable inhabitants formed the Tea Pot Club. This fund, set up in the centuries before the NHS, helped members who were sick or who needed money to pay for a funeral.

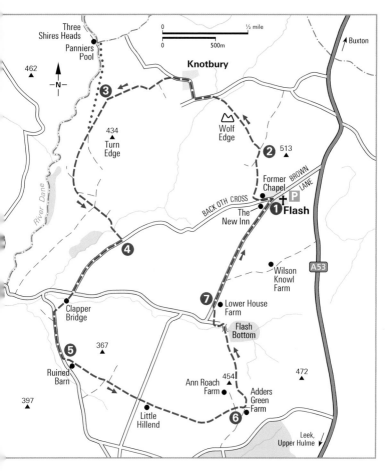

1. From the church gates walk down Back oth Cross passing the New Inn. At the edge of the village, branch right on a track bending past Bank House and Far View Cottage. Fork right at a bright yellow fingerpost and into fields. Enter a walled track, ending as you cross a stile. Continue at the edge of rough pasture, then turn left through a gate on to a short grassy track.

2. At the track's end, bear right over Wolf Edge. Descend the right boundary past a redundant stile. Cross to the far side, then cross back towards the bottom of the slope, angling down towards a lane. Go left, then right into Knotbury. Pass Knotbury Lea Cottage, then fork left at a fingerpost. Head downhill beside the wall, ignore a track left, and continue with the moorland path, bending right then left at the field end. Rise on to Turn Edge, maintaining your direction at a stile.

3. Over the crest, descend left, passing through trees to a track. Detour right here for the Panniers Pool; otherwise go left. Branch off at a tall waypost, along another falling track. Maintain a slant over rough enclosures to a gravel track. Go left to an easily missed waypost on the outside of a bend left. The grassy track runs almost parallel with, but below, the gravel track. Maintain

your direction past a gate, the way eventually steepening into a deep valley. As the track drops towards the stream, it zigzags to meet a ford. The footbridge lies to the left (not the crash-barrier bridge to the right), and is hidden by gorse; a wooden pole supporting a power cable guides you to it. Climb uphill over rough ground to a lane.

4. Turn right. At the junction, cross slightly to the right and through a squeeze stile. In wet conditions, follow the road right then left instead. Go downhill through scrub to a clapper bridge, then rise, bending gently left, across a field to a lane. Follow this uphill.

5. Near a ruined barn, fork left through a squeeze stile. Cross a pasture diagonally right, then follow a faint path across moorland grazing. Pass a building, then keep ahead on a track. Cross a lane and continue opposite through Little Hillend's driveway. A distinct, rough path leads on to the moor, eventually crossing a track from Ann Roach Farm. Cross a broken stile, through a couple of gates, and turn right to Adders Green Farm.

6. At the entrance, go left through a gate towards Flash Bottom. Follow the left wall at a corner and through a large gate. Continue ahead then bear right below a rise, the path soon descending to a plantation at Flash Bottom. Cross a footbridge then walk left up a rough track. Cross a stony driveway, taking a faint grassy path opposite towards Lower House Farm.

7. Go up steps to the road. Turn right and follow this lane gently uphill back into Flash.

Extending the walk To extend the walk to visit the Panniers Pool, turn right on the track near the start of Point 3. Return the same way, forking left at a track junction halfway.

Where to eat and drink
The Winking Man pub, a few miles down the A53 towards Upper Hulme serves good hearty food and has a range of decent ales. Walkers are welcomed and the pub is open every day of the week except Mondays.

What to see
Look for evidence of the network of packhorse trails on the moors. These routes were used from medieval times to transport goods between communities, and several of these routes converged at the Panniers Pool at Three Shires Heads. Packhorse trains could have up to 50 horses and were led by a man called a 'jagger' (their ponies were Galloway cross-breeds called Jaegers). Today you will find their paved routes descending into the valleys in distinctive 'holloways' or sunken lanes.

While you're there
Visit Buxton, England's highest market town. Founded by the Romans after they discovered a hot spring in AD 79, it became a spa town in the 18th century. Home to Buxton Spa water, there are many fine buildings, and a publicly available street fountain is still fed from St Ann's Well.

THE LIMESTONE WAY AND LATHKILL DALE

DISTANCE/TIME	9 miles (14.5km) / 5hrs
ASCENT/GRADIENT	1,085ft (331m) / ▲ ▲ ▲
PATHS	Generally well-defined paths, but limestone dale sides can be slippery after rain and there is one section of steep steps, several stiles
LANDSCAPE	Partially wooded limestone dale and open pasture
SUGGESTED MAP	OS Explorer OL24 Peak District – White Peak Area
START/FINISH	Grid reference: SK203663
DOG FRIENDLINESS	Keep on lead unless threatened by cattle
PARKING	Over Haddon pay car park
PUBLIC TOILETS	At car park

'Lathkill is, by many degrees, the purest, the most transparent stream that I ever yet saw either at home or abroad...'

Charles Cotton, 1676

Today, when you descend the winding lane into this beautiful limestone dale, you're confronted by a seemingly timeless scene of ash trees growing beneath tiered limestone crags, tumbling screes, grasslands swaying in the breeze and that same crystal-clear stream, still full of darting trout. Yet it was not always so. In the 18th and 19th centuries lead miners came here and stripped the valley of its trees. They drilled shafts and adits into the white rock, built pump houses, elaborate aqueducts, waterwheels and tramways, and when the old schemes failed to realise profits they came up with new, even bigger ones. Inevitably nobody made any real money, and by 1870 the price of lead had slumped due to overseas competition and the pistons stopped.

Your route starts on a narrow winding lane from Over Haddon to a clapper bridge by Lathkill Lodge. A lush tangle of semi-aquatic plants surrounds the river and the valley sides are thick with ash and sycamore. In the midst of the trees are some mossy pillars, the remains of an aqueduct built to supply a head of water for the nearby Mandale Mine. Further on you can cross the river to visit the remains of Bateman's House, the former mining manager's dwelling, including an underground shaft to the pumping engine (the engine is no longer visible). The path leaves the woods and the character of the dale changes again. Here, sparse ash trees grow out of the limestone screes, where herb Robert adds splashes of pink.

In summer the river may have disappeared completely beneath its bed of limestone. Emerging at the top of Lathkill Dale you reach Monyash, the halfway point of the walk, where the miners once held their special Barmote Court in The Bulls Head. The return is along the high pasture south of Lathkill, with glimpses over the dale.

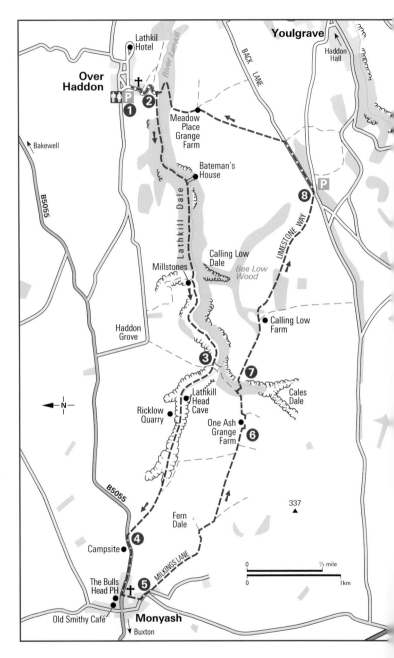

1. Turn right out of the car park then descend a narrow tarmac dead-end lane, which winds down to Lathkill Dale.

2. As the lane bends left across the river, fork right and through a gate on to a broad track to enter Lathkill Dale National Nature Reserve and the wooded dale bottom. At a footbridge it's worth crossing over to visit Bateman's House.

Pass a couple of widenings of the river (millponds), then leave the dense woodland and traverse more open, rougher slopes.

3. Ignore a junction by a footbridge and continue up the main dale. Cross the valley bottom at the mouth of Lathkill Head Cave, then weave your way through the rocky debris below Ricklow Quarry. As you approach the head of the dale, the path crosses gentle grassy fields to a road.

4. Cross the road, and take its pavement leftwards into Monyash. Go along the main street to the green with its café and pub, and turn left at the crossroads on to Rakes Road. Continue straight ahead (turning on to the side road in each case) at two close-together junctions to end up on Milkings Lane.

5. Follow this attractive walled track eastwards. Where it ends continue ahead to Fern Dale, then follow Limestone Way fingerposts across a field, then along field edges. Cross to the other side of a wall and follow the track on its far side. Eventually you drop down to join a farm track into One Ash Grange Farm.

6. Go past large farm sheds, then veer left at a track junction by the old camping barn (occasional ice cream sales in summer). Go past old pig sties then fork right to descend between more barns. Drop down through a field, then some natural limestone steps drop down below a crag. Fork right and down to a valley bottom junction. Cross over this and go up the other side of the narrow dale via a long and steep flight of steps to the top.

7. Go through a gate and head roughly southeast across fields up to Calling Low, passing through a wood to the left of the buildings then across a field and a track. Follow a waymarker diagonally across a field, pass briefly through Bee Low Wood, then across several more large fields to a lane.

8. Turn left and walk down the lane for 600yds (549m). Take a footpath left, slanting northeast across several huge fields, aiming for distant Over Haddon. At Meadow Place Grange Farm follow yellow-topped waymarkers around a wall, then across the open farmyard, exiting via gates on the far side. Head slightly right over a field to a gated track that zigzags down the wooded hillside to the river. Cross a footbridge over the Lathkill and go up the tarmac lane back to the start.

Where to eat and drink
The Old Smithy Café and The Bulls Head pub on the green at Monyash are long-standing walkers' favourites. The Lathkil Hotel, at the far eastern end of Over Haddon, is a detour at the end, but enjoys breathtaking views from its garden across the dale to Youlgrave and the White Peak (booking recommended for meals).

What to see
There are two abandoned millstones between the Lathkill millponds. Look for the grooves in the lower one – these allowed the fine milled flour to run out after grinding. The route also passes three large farmsteads – Calling Low, One Ash Grange and Meadow Place Grange. The name 'Grange' means that in medieval times they were owned by the church. The wool from their sheep was a lucrative trade and made an important contribution to monastic coffers.

ARBOR LOW
AND CALES DALE

DISTANCE/TIME	6.25 miles (10.1km) / 3hrs
ASCENT/GRADIENT	592ft (180m) / ▲
PATHS	Mostly well-defined paths, some road walking, limestone steps in Cales Dale can be very slippery when wet, a few stiles
LANDSCAPE	Limestone dales and woodland
SUGGESTED MAP	OS Explorer OL24 Peak District – White Peak Area
START/FINISH	Grid reference: SK194644
DOG FRIENDLINESS	Keep on lead on farmland, access land, country lane
PARKING	Moor Lane car park
PUBLIC TOILETS	None on route

Arbor Low is probably one of the most important prehistoric monuments in Britain. Like other mysterious stone circles, no one really knows why it was built or what function it served. Various theories suggest that it may have been a giant astronomical calculator, a religious centre, a meeting place or perhaps the earliest known supermarket.

Trading centre

Research has shown that by the late neolithic period, around about 2500 BC, complex trading networks had built up throughout Britain. Evolving from simple methods of exchange, their development mirrors the building of the henges. Throughout the Peak District axes have been discovered. These highly polished weapons were made from hard stone and originated from places as far away as North Wales, the Lake District and Northern Ireland.

Arbor Low, built near well-established trading routes, might have been the trading centre for the distribution of goods like these. The name, a corruption of the Anglo-Saxon Eorthburg Hlaw, means simply earthwork mound. It consists of a circular earthwork bank with two entrances, an internal ditch and a raised inner platform with a circle of limestone blocks. The stones may have stood upright when Arbor Low was built, but nowadays they lie flat. The passage of time may have caused them to fall over, or, as has been speculated, they were deliberately knocked over by people who knew their true purpose and significance and were afraid of them.

Ceremonial site

At the centre of the circle are the fallen stones of what is known as the cove. This, the most sacred part of the site, was made up of seven stone slabs and may have been rectangular when they were erect. No one knows what rites and ceremonies were conducted here. Only initiates would have been allowed to enter, their actions concealed from everyone else by the strategic placing of two of the larger stone slabs. During excavations the skeleton of a man was discovered in the cove, lying on his back and surrounded by blocks of stone. This is atypical of the period – the usual form of burial from that period had the knees drawn up – but reasons for the difference are unclear.

Gib Hill

Across the field to the west from Arbor Low lies a long barrow, with a round one built on top of it. The name Gib Hill suggests that it was once used for a gibbet (a gallow with a projecting arm at the top), probably in the Middle Ages. Recent research indicates that it may have been a site of execution further back in time. In the Dark Ages people feared places like Arbor Low. New, emerging rulers, anxious to establish their power, found that one way to do it was to organise executions in such places of local superstition.

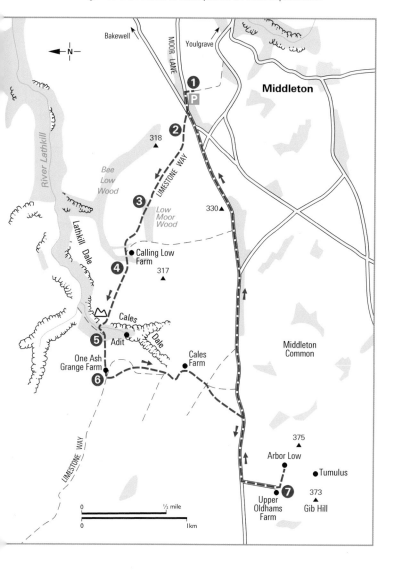

1. Exit the car park on Moor Lane, turn left and then follow the road to the T-junction. Cross the road, go through the gap in the wall, through a gate, and follow the Limestone Way across a field.

2. Bend diagonally right and cross three fields with two stiles in quick succession. Enter Low Moor Wood through a kissing gate in a stone wall.

3. Follow the path at the edge of woodland. Leave via a gate and diagonally across a field towards a farm (Calling Low). Take the diverted path right of the farm via two gates, then go through a woodland surrounding a field and three more gates to return to open meadow.

4. Follow this path downhill then bear right and downhill through fields with gates into the Lathkill Dale National Nature Reserve. Head downhill on a polished limestone path and steps. Cross a path to Lathkill Dale in the valley bottom. Rise up a short, steep slope then fork left towards One Ash Grange Farm.

5. This heads under a crag then up polished limestone steps, passing an adit on your left at the top of the steps. Keep rising on the path and through a gate into farmyard fields. Enter the farmstead via some stone steps and continue gently uphill on a stone track following yellow-topped Limestone Way markers to the right past the camping barn and to a track junction beyond a large barn.

6. Turn left on a concessionary path (not the earlier footpath), here following the farm track out past Cales Farm. At a junction of paths shortly beyond the farm bear diagonally right across fields and under a power line to the main road. Turn right and continue for 0.4 miles (600m), then turn left on to the drive for Upper Oldhams Farm, following the signs for Arbor Low.

7. Go through the farmyard following the signs. There is a small fee for using the path. Leave it in the honesty box at the farm entrance. Go through a gate, turn left along a path, then cross another stile to reach the henge. Retrace your steps to the main road, turn right, and walk about 2.5 miles (4km) back to the car park.

Where to eat and drink
Take a trip to nearby Youlgrave, which has three pubs to choose from. There's also a café within the village shop (early closing on Wednesdays).

What to see
Look for a low bank and ditch that stretch away from the southern-most of the two entrances on Arbor Low. Known as The Avenue, it may have been a ceremonial link between the two sites, but more likely it is a boundary, perhaps from the Roman period.

While you're there
You can extend your visit to Arbor Low with a short detour to Gib Hill for some fantastic views back over Arbor Low. Note the 'VR' stones around both monuments; these appear to be marker stones from when the two areas gained official protection in Queen Victoria's reign.

ACROSS STANTON MOOR

DISTANCE/TIME	4.2 miles (6.7km) / 2hrs
ASCENT/GRADIENT	575ft (175m) / ▲
PATHS	Firm moorland tracks, woodland and field paths
LANDSCAPE	Heather moorland and rolling pastoral landscapes
SUGGESTED MAP	OS Explorer OL24 Peak District – White Peak Area
START/FINISH	Grid reference: SK241624
DOG FRIENDLINESS	Keep on lead and under control; sheep on moor
PARKING	Car park opposite Birchover Stone Ltd on Birchover Road
PUBLIC TOILETS	Main Street, Birchover

Stanton Moor is a small and distinctive upthrust of gritstone amid the limestone dales of the White Peak, where heather and silver birch provide a marked contrast to the rolling pasture and undulating river valleys all around. To the east it looks down on to the Derwent Valley and Matlock, while to the west there are panoramic views to Bakewell and the valley of the River Wye.

Dancing on the sabbath

The whole of the moor is a Scheduled Ancient Monument (a legally protected site due to its historical importance), dotted with dozens of ancient cairns, barrows and tumuli, although much of it is hidden by heather, gorse and bilberry. Since the Bronze Age, settlers have favoured the moor for the protection that this high vantage point must have offered. However, its association with druids and ritual worship has made Stanton Moor particularly well known. Nine Ladies stone circle, situated in a clearing of silver birch, has nine stones, which are supposed to represent women who were caught dancing on the sabbath and turned to stone. The King Stone, set back from the circle, is the unfortunate fiddler. Antiquarians over the centuries have made much of Stanton Moor as a magnet for druidical activity, with the bizarre rock carvings at Rowtor Rocks interpreted as sacrificial basins, altars and rock cells for ungodly practices. Although there's little evidence of ritual worship and human sacrifice, the moor exudes an air of mystery that makes it a great place to explore.

Gritstone blocks and towers

On the route across the moor you will pass several giant blocks of gritstone standing isolated among the heather. Many of these blocks around the moors have their own name, such as the Cork Stone, Heart Stone, Twopenny Loaf (Andle Stone) and the Cat Stone. They are all natural lumps of stone, weathered into fantastic shapes. Some believe that they were once probably objects of pagan worship, although now their devotees are usually climbers who use them for 'bouldering'. Along the eastern edge of the moor you'll pass

Earl Grey Tower. This folly was built by the Thornhill family to celebrate the passing of Grey's historic Reform Bill in 1832 which gave middle-class men the vote.

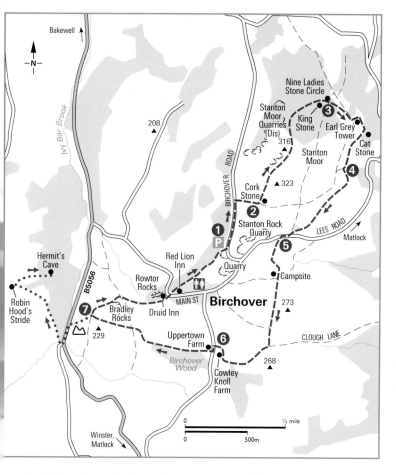

1. Head left on the road and past the quarry entrance. After a quarter of a mile (400m) turn right for a signposted path on to the moor.

2. Go through a gate then fork directly left at the Cork Stone. This quickly becomes a wide track across the middle of the heather moor (ignore narrower paths to either side). Stay on the wide path as it enters silver birch scrub, then near a fence ahead, in a slight clearing, fork right on to a wide grassy track. Fork right at a corner of fencing then pass the King Stone and Nine Ladies.

3. From the interpretation panel at the stone circle, take a wide path directly opposite. Maintain your direction ahead at a split in the track; the wide sandy path leads to the Earl Grey Tower. Cross the stile then go down a set of stone steps on the far side of the tower. Keep a fenceline on your right on a narrow woodland path through Stanton Moor Edge. Detour left briefly at a corner for the Cat Stone or stay right with the fence for the main path.

4. Cross over a stile by a National Trust sign, then fork left and gently away from the fenceline. Turn left at a track junction, and go downhill to the road. Turn right, then take the next (signed) footpath on your left.

5. Follow this path beside a campsite, turn left by some buildings then right at Hill Carr Barn. A constrained grassy track squeezes through a stile then you follow the right-hand edge of two fields to meet the unsurfaced Clough Lane. Turn right along this and down to Cowley Knoll Farm.

6. Turn left on to a surfaced lane, then almost immediately right, by Uppertown Farm. The gated track leads to a path along the left edge of fields. Then, after hugging a wall on the right, the path continues past a cottage and begins a huge loop around a hilly outcrop and plantation. At the far end go through a gate and descend by a wire fence, bending right to the bottom of the plantation.

7. For the walk extension fork left and downhill. Otherwise, continue with the level track as it swings back towards Birchover. Join a gravel drive on a bend, take the lower route, then cross a junction, heading past The Old Vicarage. (For Rowtor Rocks, look for a narrow path on the left opposite The Old Vicarage.) At the road take the signposted footpath by the Millennium Stone (opposite the pub). Rise up along a wooded ridge back to the car park.

Extending the walk You can extend this walk at Point 7 to visit Robin Hood's Stride and the Hermit's Cave (dating from the 14th century, with a crucifix carved on its wall). Follow the path steeply down to the road in the valley bottom, turn left and cross over for the path that takes you up to the rocks. Return the same way.

Where to eat and drink
Birchover has two good pubs. The Red Lion Inn is a traditional village local which has been restored its historical status of a micro-brewery and a serves a varied daily menu. Open all day at weekends, closed Monday and Tuesday. The Druid Inn offers changing choices of real ale and a menu utilising many local ingredients. Open all day in summer and at lunchtimes in the winter.

What to see
In this area of rocky outcrops, Rowtor Rocks is certainly one of the most intriguing. You reach it up a narrow path behind the Druid Inn, and amid the jumble of huge gritstone blocks you will find rocking stones, excavated holes and caves, narrow staircases, basins and seats all carved out of the bare rock.

While you're there
Robin Hood's Stride is a distinctive group of gritstone rocks on the skyline between Birchover and Youlgrave – Robin is said to have leapt from one stone to the other in one stride. It also goes by the name of Mock Beggars' Hall, since from a distance its two rock towers resemble tall chimneys.

THE ROACHES

DISTANCE/TIME	3.8 miles (6km) / 2hrs
ASCENT/GRADIENT	625ft (191m) / ▲
PATHS	Rocky moorland paths, forest tracks and road
LANDSCAPE	Moor and woodland
SUGGESTED MAP	OS Explorer OL24 Peak District – White Peak Area
START/FINISH	Grid reference: SK004621
DOG FRIENDLINESS	Access land, keep on lead
PARKING	In lay-by on lane below The Roaches
PUBLIC TOILETS	None on route
NOTES	This route was ravaged by wildfire in 2018. It is hoped that the outstanding natural beauty of this area will recover to some degree, but it may take a few years to return to its former glory

The jagged ridge of The Roaches is one of the most popular outdoor locations in the Peak District National Park. The name is a corruption of the French for rocks: *roches*. It was here on the gritstone crags that the 'working-class revolution' in climbing took place in the 1950s. Manchester lads Joe Brown, a builder, and Don Whillans, a plumber, went on to become legends within the climbing fraternity by developing new rock-climbing techniques wearing gym shoes and using Joe's mother's discarded clothes line as a rope.

Natural cave-dwelling

Look out for Rockhall Cottage, built into the rock and containing at least one room that is a natural cave. The cottage was a former gamekeeper's residence and is currently owned by the Peak District National Park. Restored in 1989, and now known as the Don Whillans Memorial Hut, the bothy can be booked through the British Mountaineering Council by small groups of climbers. Otherwise, you can glimpse the listed building from a distance.

Jenny Greenteeth and Doxey Pool

Other less tangible legends surround this long outcrop, several of them attached to Doxey Pool. Locals speak in hushed voices of a young mermaid who lived in the pool but was captured by a group of men. If the stories are to be believed, her ghost can still be heard singing through the mist. Lurking in the darkest depths of the pool is Jenny Greenteeth, a hideous monster with green skin, long hair and sharp teeth, who grabs the ankles of anyone unfortunate enough to get too close, dragging them to a watery grave. Another myth says the pool is bottomless and will never dry out. Sadly this myth was busted in the heatwave of 2018, when it did indeed dry out, leaving little but damp peat on its surface.

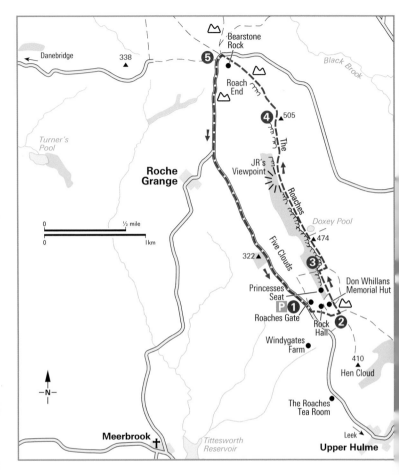

1. Descend the lane from the long parking lay-by below The Roaches. Turn left through the main gate into access land, by the interpretation panel at Roaches Gate. Follow the main path which gently rises to the southern end of the rocks. On the way there are a couple of tracks which lead left to Rock Hall, but ignore all side turns until you reach a crossing track. (This leads to the top of the angular cliff wall of Hen Cloud on your right.)

2. Fork left on to a broad rocky track to begin the ascent to The Roaches ridgeline. Take the next fork left on to a narrower sandy track leading between two distinct levels of rock crags. Go left through a pair of stone gateposts and continue right on a well-defined track. The path is flanked by rocks on the right and woodland to the left and below. Follow it under the rocks to a sandy T-junction.

3. Turn right and rise up a stepped path through a gap in the rocks to the ridgeline. Turn left and follow the ridge path, passing to the left of Doxey Pool. Look out for JR's viewpoint with its fabulous views as far as the North Wales hills on a very clear day. It's roughly halfway between Doxey Pool and the trig point.

4. From the trig point summit, descend on a sandy path through bouldery rocks. As the outcrops fade, this becomes an easy-going paved path. Continue past the Bearstone Rock, to join the road at Roach End.

5. Turn left down the road, pass through a gate, and go back to the start point.

Where to eat and drink

The Roaches Tea Room at Paddock Farm sits beneath the rocky outcrop of Hen Cloud, just down the road towards Leek. There's a conservatory overlooking a herb garden and superb views across Tittesworth Reservoir. It's open daily all year. Ye Olde Rock Inn at Upper Hulme also does great bar meals and real ale.

What to see

Part way along the ridgeline, look out for a small grassy ledge with a fantastic viewpoint. The rock at the back of the ledge is inscribed with the initials JR carved with a degree of skill into the rock. From here you can see as far as The Wrekin on a clear day, with nearer landmarks such as Croker Hill (with its transmitter), Jodrell Bank and Tittesworth Reservoir.

While you're there

Leek is a magnet for antiques hunters. As well as having a host of antiques dealers, there's an open-air craft and antiques market each Saturday in the historic Market Square. Other markets include the Butter Market, selling mainly fresh traditional produce, on Wednesday, Friday and Saturday.

35 AROUND TITTESWORTH WATER

DISTANCE/TIME	4.5 miles (7.2km) / 2hrs 30min
ASCENT/GRADIENT	345ft (105m) / ▲
PATHS	Good well-made footpaths, forest tracks and roads
LANDSCAPE	Reservoir and woodland
SUGGESTED MAP	OS Explorer OL24 Peak District – White Peak Area
START/FINISH	Grid reference: SJ993601
DOG FRIENDLINESS	On lead at all times and under control
PARKING	Tittesworth Water Visitor Centre (pay car park)
PUBLIC TOILETS	At Tittesworth Water Visitor Centre

Tittesworth Water and dam were built in 1858 to collect water from the River Churnet and provide a reliable water supply to Leek's thriving textile and cloth-dying industry. By 1963 work to increase its size had been completed, and local farmland was flooded to create a reservoir capable of supplying drinking water to Stoke-on-Trent and the surrounding areas. With a capacity of 6.5 billion gallons (29.5 billion litres), when full it can supply 10 million gallons (45.5 million litres) of water every day.

The land around the reservoir provides a habitat for a wide variety of wildlife, and many creatures can be seen in the course of this walk. Look out for brown hares in the fields near the car park. You can tell them from rabbits by their very long legs, black-tipped ears and a triangular black and light brown tail. Otters were once hunted almost to extinction by dogs, and although the sport is now illegal their numbers remain low, but look out for the tell-tale prints of their webbed feet and wavy line of tail prints in the sand and soft mud. Look also for holes in the banks along the River Churnet, where otters enter the reservoir. Although it's a difficult little creature to spot, a hole may just be the entrance to a vole burrow and home to a water vole like Ratty from *The Wind in the Willows*.

Europe's smallest bat, the pipistrelle, suffered a severe decline in numbers in the last decades of the 20th century due to loss of hunting habitats like hedges, ponds and grassland. Pond restoration near Churnet Bay is encouraging their return and they can best be seen here near dusk, flying at an incredible speed as they dive to gobble caddisflies, moths and gnats. Bird life around the reservoir is also abundant and there are two bird hides for visitors' use. Look out for skylarks, small birds with a high-pitched continuous warble, that nest in the meadows around Tittesworth. The song thrush, another bird that has been in decline, also finds a home here, as does the linnet. Look for the male of the species in spring and summer when it has a bright blood-red breast and forehead. At various times of the year you might spot barnacle geese, great crested grebes, pied flycatchers, spectacular kingfishers, cormorants and even a rare osprey that has visited here.

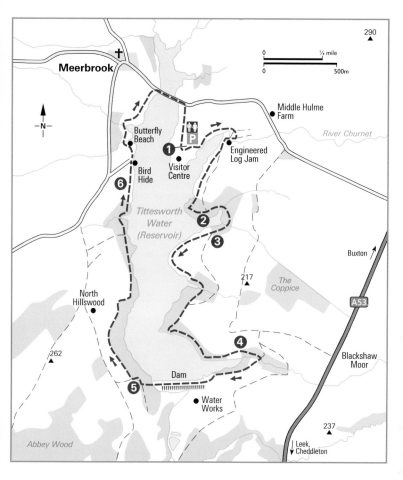

1. Facing the entrance to the Visitor Centre cross the car park to your left and follow a path signed 'Waymarked Walks'. Bend left at an early junction then pass the main car park and a play area. Ignore side paths on a twisty section to pass an engineered 'log jam' then cross two bridges. Fork right from the main trail to take the 'Water's edge path'. Ignore all side turns along this, bending left at a small headland and past some woodland. Now bend left into the woods and fork right at a track junction to rejoin the 'Long Trail' (unsigned).

2. Follow the Long Trail through the wood, crossing two small bridges. As the path leaves the wood fork right on to a grassy track, again signed 'Water's edge path'.

3. Continue along the bank of the reservoir, then re-enter the woodland and cross some duckboards. Cross a bridge by a picnic table, ascend some steps and turn right to rejoin the wide main track once more. Skirt the edge of a wood, keeping a fence on your left, then go downhill through a wood and along the reservoir bank before rising back into thin woodland.

4. Pass a 3km waymarker on a slight rise in the track, then cross a bridge. Rise steeply uphill on a graded track (replacing older steps), staying on the main path as a path joins from a field. Go downhill towards the dam wall on a graded path (again passing older steps) and take the footway across the dam wall. Climb up steps beside a woodland conservation area, then turn right on to a track, which soon bends left to a junction.

5. Bend right here, staying on the 'long trail'. This keeps just right of fields, bending right and briefly downhill into undulating woodland and passing a 5km waymarker. Cross some metal-grilled boardwalks either side of a bridge, then head up over a small knoll of mixed woodland. This is followed by steps either side of a boardwalk bridge.

6. As you exit woodland you gain a pleasant view over Hen Cloud and The Roaches ahead. Stay on the stone path beside a wildflower meadow. Join the end of a tarmac road past the watersports centre, then cross over a junction by a metal barrier and open bird hide. The wide gravel path ahead leads past the Butterfly Beach, then out to the main road. Turn right along the grass verge then right on to a tarmac path running alongside the Visitor Centre driveway to return to the start.

Where to eat and drink
Stop at the Tittesworth Water Visitor Centre and its light and airy restaurant has great views over the water. It offers a good selection of food options, ranging from a full breakfast to local specialities such as Staffordshire oatcakes, and from hot paninis to afternoon teas with delicious scones and pastries.

What to see
Look out for a couple of unusual experimental areas. There's an engineered 'log jam' near the start which is testing a way of reducing flooding risk in rivers. Towards the end of the walk, Butterfly Beach is designed to encourage breeding butterflies. This 'luxury hotel' for these delightful insects has a sandy beach for a spot of sunbathing on a warm summer day, and thistles, nettles and a host of wild flowers to provide egg-laying sites and food.

While you're there
Visit the Churnet Valley Railway for a magical trip back to the 1950s and 1960s on a preserved steam railway, which meanders along beside the River Churnet and the Caldon Canal. If you're trying to entertain the kids – look out for special children's weekends in summer. These may include offers where those dressing up to match the theme (e.g. Superheroes and Princesses) go free, or close encounters with unusual animals whose handlers come to the stations to bring alive the wonders of the natural world.

36

HARTINGTON AND
THE UPPER DOVE VALLEY

DISTANCE/TIME	7.8 miles (12.6km) / 4hrs
ASCENT/GRADIENT	950ft (290m) / ▲ ▲
PATHS	Field paths and lanes, some steep climbs, ascent from Crowdecote and descent to Hartington can be very slippery in wet conditions, many stiles
LANDSCAPE	Pastures and limestone valley
SUGGESTED MAP	OS Explorer OL24 Peak District – White Peak Area
START/FINISH	Grid reference: SK127602
DOG FRIENDLINESS	Keep dogs on lead; metal-grilled footpath
PARKING	Parson's Field pay car park in Hartington
PUBLIC TOILETS	Opposite side of road to car park
NOTES	Ancient mine shafts on access land near Carder Low may not be fenced off

Hartington, lying in the mid-regions of the Dove Valley, is a prosperous village with 18th-century houses and hotels built in local limestone and lined around spacious greens. Its history can be traced back to the Normans, when it was recorded as Hartedun, the centre of the De Ferrier's Estate. Hartington Hall, now a youth hostel, was first built in 1350, but was substantially rebuilt in 1611. Bonnie Prince Charlie is reputed to have stopped here in 1745 on his march into Derby, where 5,000 Highland troops were amassing to fight for the Jacobite cause. He didn't know that the Duke of Devonshire had amassed 30,000 loyalists.

Pilsbury Castle

Pilsbury Castle hides from view until the very last moment, but then a grassy ramp swoops down to it from the hillsides. Only the earthworks are now visible; you can see the motte, a man-made mound built to accommodate the wooden keep, and the bailey, a raised embankment that would have had a wooden stockade round it. The castle's exact history is disputed. It was probably built around 1100 by the Normans, on the site of an Iron Age fort. It may have been a stronghold used earlier by William I to suppress a local rebellion in his 'Wasting of the North' campaign. Being in the middle of the De Ferrier Estate it was probably their administrative centre. In the 1200s this function would have been moved to Hartington. Views up the valley are fascinating, with the sharp limestone ridges of the Parkhouse and Chrome Hills in the distance. Now the route descends into Dovedale for the first time, crossing the river into Staffordshire and climbs to a high lane running the length of the dale's east rim. Note the change in the rock: it's now the darker gritstone. Now you can see for miles, across the Manifold Valley to The Roaches and Hen Cloud, before Sheen Hill blocks the view. A field path takes the route on its finale, descending along a line of crags with lofty views.

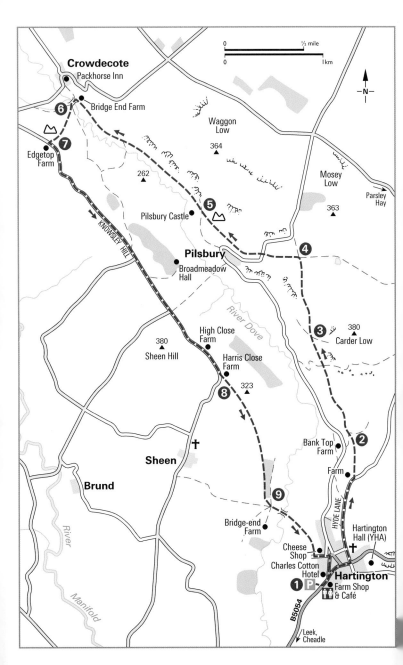

1. Turn left out of the car park and follow the road, curving right through the centre of the village. Turn left on to Hyde Lane. After half a mile (800m), and just after a large barn, fork left towards Pilsbury and Crowdecote over a step-stile and into fields. Follow waymarkers across three fields, then at the start of the fourth swing left beside a dry-stone wall.

2. Go through a white-painted gateway and on to a concrete track, which you follow down to a sharp bend. Leave the track here, continuing straight ahead back into fields. Initially stay near the top wall, then across the open hillside. The path is well marked with occasional white-painted posts and crossing stiles.

3. Meet a track by a clump of trees, go through a gate, cross the track, then maintain your direction on a footpath towards Pilsbury and Crowdecote. This again is well signed across fields with yellow-topped fingerposts. Cross a faint farm track then descend into a small grassy valley.

4. Fork left in the valley bottom on a grassy path. Cross a lane by a barn and across fields to Crowdecote, passing just right of a breezeblock hut then beside a stone wall. Suddenly, Pilsbury Castle comes into view, the path then raking down to a track and a kissing gate into the castle enclosure.

5. A grassy track leads right downhill and out of the enclosure to continue along the valley bottom across successive pastures. A developing track eventually leads to Bridge End Farm.

6. Turn left just after a farm silo to cross the River Dove by a little footbridge. Follow the path directly uphill across a field.

7. Beyond the wall stile the path veers right, through scrub, to reach the Longnor Road near Edge Top. After heavy rain and in winter you may wish to stay on the Longnor Road from Crowdecote, otherwise turn left along the high lane, reaching High Close Farm after roughly 1.75 miles (2.8km). Keep going to a bend right in the road.

8. Turn left at this bend into a farm driveway (Harris Close Farm). There's an 1842 plaque near the top of the house wall. Immediately as you enter the yard, head for the far right of a barn and over a stile. Follow the right wall across successive fields, keeping ahead beyond its end. After going through a small pine plantation, bear left to descend through scrub to the valley. Turn right along a farm track.

9. Take the next gate left and directly across a field to a footbridge across the Dove. Bear right to a gate and follow a diagonal route across several fields. Enter woodland (now screening modern housing built on the former creamery) by a gate and continue at the edge of a final field to a lane. Turn left back to Hartington, then right at the Market Square to the car park.

Where to eat and drink
Excellent meals are served at the Charles Cotton Hotel in Hartington and at the Packhorse Inn (closed Monday and Tuesday) at Crowdecote. Hartington Farm Shop and Café is just opposite the car park. It serves breakfast and a range of lunches and snacks. Closed Mondays.

What to see
In Hartington, The Old Cheese Shop sells Stilton cheese, once again made in the parish, following the closure of the original Dairy Crest Creamery. Below Pilsbury, look out for Broadmeadow Hall, a 17th-century manor house which was the administrative centre of the region under the Sleigh family in the early 18th century.

MATLOCK BATH AND THE HEIGHTS OF ABRAHAM

DISTANCE/TIME	4.7 miles (7.6km) / 3hrs
ASCENT/GRADIENT	1,230ft (375m) / ▲ ▲
PATHS	Narrow limestone woodland paths, field paths, stone tracks and tarmac lanes, may be muddy, several stiles
LANDSCAPE	Fields and wooded hillsides
SUGGESTED MAP	OS Explorer OL24 Peak District – White Peak Area
START/FINISH	Grid reference: SK297595
DOG FRIENDLINESS	Dogs on lead on farmland and access land; usual controls in town
PARKING	Pay car park at Artists Corner
PUBLIC TOILETS	In Bonsall and near bridge to Matlock Bath railway station

Between Matlock and Cromford the River Derwent forges its way through a spectacular, wooded limestone gorge. At Matlock Bath it jostles for space with the A6 highway, the railway to Derby and a string of three-storey houses, shops and amusement parlours. On the hillside to the east lies the gaunt castle of Riber, while Alpine-type cable cars glide up the Heights of Abraham.

The original Heights of Abraham, which the hillside must have resembled, rise above Quebec and the St Lawrence River in Canada. There, in 1759, British troops under General Wolfe fought a victorious battle with the French under the Marquis de Montcalm. Both generals were killed and the encounter earned Wolfe, and Quebec, an unenviable place in English place-name folklore, to be joined later by Waterloo and, later still, Spion Kop.

Matlock Bath is like Derbyshire's mini-Blackpool. Yet there are peaceful corners, and this walk seeks them out. It offers fine views across the Matlock Gorge. Spurning the cable car, it climbs through the woods and out on to the hillside above the town. The Victoria Prospect Tower peeps over the trees. Built by unemployed miners a century ago, it's now part of the Heights of Abraham complex. Above the complex, a little path leads you through delectable woodland. In spring it's heavy with the scent of wild garlic and coloured by a carpet of bluebells. Out of the woods, an attractive hedge-lined unsurfaced lane weaves its way through high pastures, giving distant views of the White Peak plateau, Black Rocks and the cliffs of Crich Stand.

At the end of the lane, there's Bonsall, whose Perpendicular church tower and spire have been beckoning you onwards for some time. In the centre of this old lead-mining village is a sloping market square with a 17th-century cross. The Kings Head Inn, built in 1677, overlooks the square, and is said to be haunted. The lane out of Bonsall takes you to the edge of an area of old mine shafts and modern-day quarries. Here you're diverted into the woods above the Via Gellia, a valley named after Philip Gell, who built the road from the quarry to the Cromford Canal. Those who wish can make a short diversion from the woodland path to see the Cromford Mills (site of Richard Arkwright's first mill complex) and canal. The main route swings north, back into the woods of the Derwent Valley, passing the high hamlet of Upperwood, where fleeting views of Matlock appear through the trees.

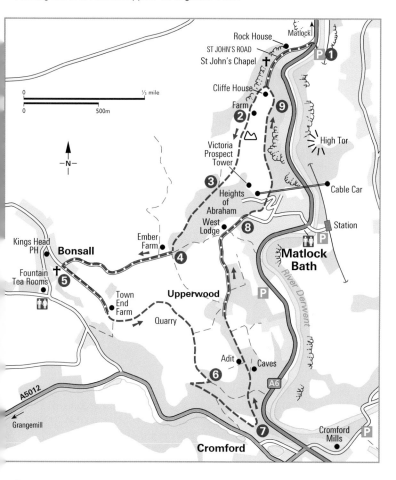

1. From the north end of the car park, cross the A6 and take St John's Road up the wooded slopes opposite. Fork right as the road divides, heading uphill and below St John's Chapel to the gates of Cliffe House. Take a footpath immediately right of the gates; this climbs steeply through the woods before running along the field edge above a farm.

2. As views open out directly opposite Riber Castle, and with Victoria Prospect Tower directly ahead, the waymarked path swings right and climbs up to the top of the field. The footpath threads through mixed deciduous woodland (which can be muddy underfoot if wet) and a grassy field, before reaching one of the entrances to the Heights of Abraham complex.

3. Ignore an obvious, engineered path and continue briefly uphill beside the perimeter wall to a gate. Pass through, cross a wide vehicle track and carry on through woodland.

4. At the far side of the woods, turn right on to a farm track close to Ember Farm. This becomes a pretty lane that winds down pastured hillslopes into Bonsall.

5. Turn left by the church along a lane that becomes unsurfaced when you get beyond Town End Farm. Curving left, the track skirts the high fence of a quarry. Later narrowing to a path, it descends to the right into trees.

6. A brief clearing leads to a wider expanse of woodland. After a few paces, bend sharp right with the quarry fenceline, falling on a narrow path through woodland high above the Via Gellia. Stay with the fenceline heading right at a junction by a sharp fence corner then continue on a narrower path next to a derelict post and rail fence. This descends gently above Cromford. Ignore a path fork by an old gatepost and descend to the next fork (above a small wooden shed).

7. Turn left here (waymarked) to stay on the route, passing above houses – or detour ahead to Cromford if you wish. Fork left at a junction on a small spur, soon following a low wall on the right. Pass above a disused tennis court, then fork left. Continue ahead past a junction by an adit. At the edge of woodland, fork left on to a grassy track that soon becomes a lane. This descends through Upperwood, passing West Lodge, the main entrance to the Heights of Abraham.

8. Just before a sharp bend right in the road, fork left on to a stepped path through the woods on the left, signed 'To Matlock'. Climb steps to a wooden footbridge over a lane, and continue on the woodland path. You'll pass under the Heights of Abraham cable cars before joining a farm track that comes in from the left.

9. This joins St John's Road and the initial outward route at Cliffe House. Retrace your steps to the start.

Where to eat and drink

The Kings Head at Bonsall is known for good bar meals. Alternatively, you could try the Fountain Tea Rooms (or the next-door stores and deli for a takeaway snack at the bottom of Yeoman Street). The 17th-century Barley Mow in Bonsall is also very popular but is some distance off-route.

What to see

St John's Chapel was designed and built in 1897 by Sir Guy Dauber for Mrs Harris, who lived at Rock House. It was meant to serve the parishioners who found it difficult to reach St Giles at Matlock, but it also was a place for those worshippers who preferred a High Church service. Contact Friends of the Friendless Churches for access details.

While you're there

Explore the Heights of Abraham by taking the Alpine-style cable car, built in 1984. Included in the fare are the show caves (no dogs). There's also an interpretation centre and a café in the complex.

CROMFORD AND THE BLACK ROCKS

DISTANCE/TIME	9 miles (14.5km) / 5hrs
ASCENT/GRADIENT	1,445ft (440m) / ▲ ▲ ▲
PATHS	Lanes and urban ginnels, woodland and field paths, canal towpath and a former railway trackbed, several stiles
LANDSCAPE	Town streets, wooded hillsides and grassy valleysides
SUGGESTED MAP	OS Explorer OL24 Peak District – White Peak Area
START/FINISH	Grid reference: SK300570
DOG FRIENDLINESS	Under close control at all times; keep out of the canal to protect water voles
PARKING	Cromford Wharf pay car park
PUBLIC TOILETS	At car park and High Peak junction

For many centuries Cromford, 'the ford by the bend in the river', was no more than a sleepy backwater. Everything changed in 1771 when Sir Richard Arkwright decided to build the world's first water-powered cotton-spinning mill here. Within 20 years he had built two more, and had constructed a whole town around them. As you walk through the restored courtyard of the Cromford Mills you are transported back into that austere world of the 18th century. Most of the town lies on the other side of the traffic-laden A6, including the mill pond which was built by Arkwright to impound the waters of Bonsall Brook, and the beautifully restored mill workers' cottages of North Street.

The Black Rocks overlook the town from the south. The walk makes a beeline for them through little ginnels (alleys), past some almshouses and through pine woods. You'll see climbers grappling with the 80ft (24m) gritstone crags, but there's a good path all the way to the top where you can look across the Derwent Valley.

The next stage of the journey takes you on to the High Peak Trail, which uses the former trackbed of the Cromford and High Peak Railway. Engineered by Josias Jessop and constructed in the 1830s, the railway was built as an extension of the canal system and, as such, the stations were called wharves. In the early years horses pulled the wagons on the level stretches, while steam-winding engines worked the inclines. By the mid-1800s horses were replaced by steam locomotives. The south end of the line connected with the newly extended Midland Railway. The railway was closed by Dr Beeching in 1967. The walk now swings south through high woods and fields above the Derwent Valley before crossing the river at Whatstandwell and returning via the towpath of the disused Cromford Canal. The 33-mile (53km) canal was built in 1793 to provide a navigable waterway to the River Trent via the Erewash. The final section of the walk is via Bow Wood, west of Lea Bridge. It's an area of beautiful woodland that must have once covered the valley sides.

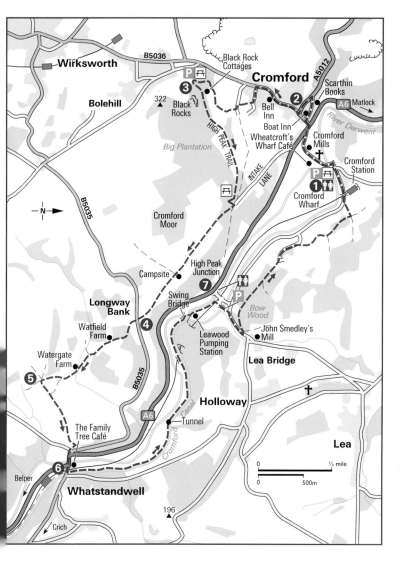

1. Turn left from the car park and up to the A6 junction. Cross over the busy road, then take the first right (towards Scarthin Books shop) passing the old mill-pond, before doubling back left at a T-junction to Market Place.

2. Turn right up The Hill. Pass North Street, then ignore a footpath left. Take the next left up Bedehouse Lane, which bends right into a narrow tarmac walkway. Cross a road and take a footpath towards Black Rocks. At its top, turn left up a steep and winding lane. Higher up, take the right-most tarmac footpath, crossing a cattle grid and rising to the Black Rock Cottages ahead. Fork right along the top of a field. Climb a few steps to pass round the fenced-off Black Rocks Scree Slope then take a trail into the woods opposite an information sign. Head uphill to the High Peak Trail.

3. Turn left towards High Peak Junction. Pass Sheep Pasture engine house and go down the first part of the incline. Turn right towards Intake Lane, bend left, ignore a concessionary path to the right, and go down to a waymarked junction. Turn right towards Longway Bank, rising on the wide woodland track. At the edge of the wood fork right and pass a gate. Turn left on to a stony track, pass a large campsite, then bend right and up to a road.

4. Cross this and take a rising footpath through a field. Fork left below Crabtree Wood, then rise steeply through a hilltop plantation, with boardwalk across boggier parts. Keep left of some buildings (Watfield Farm), joining a stony lane at the bottom of the driveway. Fork right by woods on to a footpath which heads downhill past Watergate Farm. Cross the driveway and follow waymarkers uphill through fields to a hilly junction.

5. Turn left on a field-edge path, and down to pass just right of a cottage. The path steepens by a wooden fence, crosses a driveway, then descends to a road. Cross a small field then the River Derwent via the A6 bridge. Fork left by The Family Tree café on to the Crich road, then turn left on to the Cromford Canal towpath.

6. Follow this for about 2 miles (3.2km), including a short tunnel (there's an alternative path over the top). When the chimney of Lea Wood pumping station comes into view, switch banks via the swingbridge.

7. At High Peak Junction swingbridge, turn right on to a fenced path. Take a road pavement to the right, entering Lea Bridge. Just before John Smedley's Mill turn sharp left on to a footpath through Bow Wood. Join a tarmac lane on a hairpin bend and head downhill. Just after an overhead power line, fork right on to a footpath, rising gently across open pasture. Go through a wood then head left down a stepped path to the road. Turn right to return to Cromford Wharf.

Where to eat and drink
The Wheatcroft's Wharf Café at the end of the Cromford Canal and Arkwright's Café (in the mill complex) are popular walkers' choices, or try the small vegetarian café above Scarthin Books. The Boat Inn is an excellent pub in Cromford. Part-way around the route, The Family Tree licensed café has a large outside garden and a wide choice of food and drinks.

What to see
Besides Arkwright's Cromford Mills, which is a 'must see', look out for a waterwheel on your left on the way back to the millpond, which was used for crushing local ore to produce pigments for paint. As you pass The Bell, look out for the historic millworkers' cottages on North Street. Visit the exhibits in old railway workshops at High Peak Junction and, if open (limited days), visit the historic Leawood Pumping Station.

While you're there
If you have time, visit Wirksworth, a former lead-mining town on the hillside above Cromford.

WOLFSCOTE DALE AND BIGGIN DALE

DISTANCE/TIME	8 miles (12.9km) / 4hrs 30min
ASCENT/GRADIENT	1,020ft (311m) / ▲
PATHS	Generally well-defined paths, although the limestone dale can be slippery after rain
LANDSCAPE	Partially wooded limestone dales and high pasture
SUGGESTED MAP	OS Explorer OL24 Peak District – White Peak Area
START/FINISH	Grid reference: SK156548
DOG FRIENDLINESS	On lead in dales (nature reserve); under close control elsewhere – avoid long stretchy leads on trail to prevent tripping other users
PARKING	Alsop Station pay car park
PUBLIC TOILETS	None on route

From its source, on Axe Edge, to Hartington, the River Dove is little more than a stream flowing past the Dragon's Back at Chrome Hill, and in an attractive but shallow valley south of Crowdecote. But once through the pretty woodlands of Beresford Dale it cuts a deep limestone canyon with cliffs and tors almost equal to those of the more celebrated Dovedale. This canyon is Wolfscote Dale, and it's wilder and more unspoiled than Dovedale, with narrower, less populated paths, and less woodland to hide the crags. Weirs have been constructed along the river that attract trout and grayling to linger.

Early remains

There are several small caves high up amid the soaring limestone peaks along this stretch of the Dove. Formed by the effects of water, which gouged out the rock as the glaciers melted in the latter stages of the last Ice Age, they would have offered shelter for early hunters and later some of them were used as tombs for family and tribal members. A few, such as Reynard's Cave further downstream, have yielded various artefacts.

Wolfscote Dale

The path up Wolfscote Dale begins at Lode Mill. The whole of Wolfscote and Biggin Dales are part of the Dove Valley National Nature Reserve, known for its many species of limestone-loving plants and its butterflies. The river, verged by lush vegetation, has cut a deep and twisting valley through the limestone. The slopes are thickly wooded with ash, sycamore and alder. Further north this woodland thins out to reveal more of the crags, and a ravine opens out to the right of Coldeaton Bridge. The dale, like so many in Derbyshire, is rich in wildlife. The dale divides again beneath the magnificent Peaseland Rocks. Biggin Dale follows, and for most of the year it's a dry valley, but in winter the rocky path may be jostling for room with a newly surfaced stream. It's a narrow dale with limestone screes and scrub gorse. What looks like a natural cave over a stile to the right is in fact the entrance to an old lead mine. At the top of the dale you come to Biggin, a straggling village, from where the return route is an easy-paced one using the Tissington Trail, which ambles over the high plains of Alsop Moor.

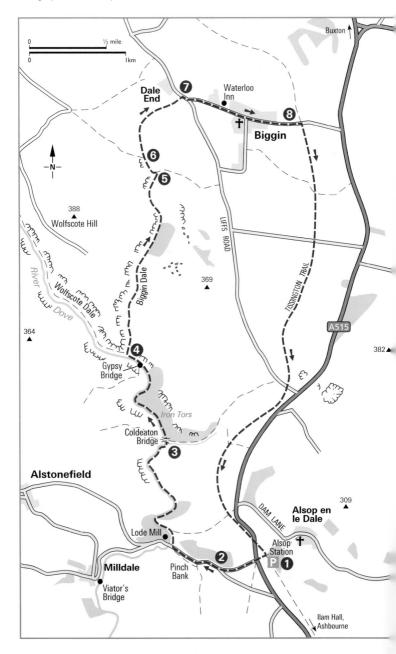

1. From the car park, carefully cross the busy A515 road and follow the lane opposite signed to Mill Dale.

2. Go right at a junction, and follow the lane down to the bridge at Lode Mill. (If the road is particularly popular, as sometimes happens in summer, part-way down on the left there's an alternative road-avoiding path. However it's narrow and sometimes overgrown so the road is best when clear.) Turn right just before the bridge and to the path running alongside the river.

3. Stay on the path beside the river at both a shuttered building and Coldeaton Bridge, continuing beneath thickly wooded slopes on the right. Beyond Gypsy Bridge and a squeeze stile, the woods cease and the dale becomes bare and rock-fringed, overlooked by the bold pinnacles of Peaseland Rocks ahead.

4. Go through a gate in the wall and immediately turn right, up the dry valley of Biggin Dale, and continue beneath steep gorse-covered limestone banks and screes, passing through a gate into woodland.

5. Where the dale broadens out and divides there's a path junction with a concrete dew pond over the wall on the left. Turn left, signposted 'Hartington', and once through a gate swing right following the valley waymarkers.

6. At the next junction of paths, stay with the valley as it bends right at a wall, following the path to Biggin. Pass an unusual small reed-bed water treatment works then climb out of the dale to reach the road at Dale End.

7. Turn right along the road for a few paces then bear left, following a road past the Waterloo Inn and through Biggin village.

8. Continue up the road to the old railway bridge where you join the Tissington Trail. Follow this old trackbed southwards across the pastures of Biggin and Alport Moors. After 3 miles (4.8km) you reach the car park at the former Alsop Station.

Where to eat and drink

The Waterloo Inn at Biggin is an ideal place for a break before heading back to Alsop. Enjoy a meal or bar snack in the large south facing beer garden or even grab a takeaway.

What to see

In Biggin Dale, besides the rampantly prickly gorse bushes, you should see many limestone-loving plants, including the purple-flowered meadow cranesbill, patches of delicate harebells, early purple orchids with their dark-spotted stems and leaves, and cheerful yellow cowslips.

While you're there

A bit further down Dovedale are the famous Viator's Bridge at Milldale, and then the stepping stones. Also try Ilam Hall (National Trust), which has plenty of options to keep children entertained.

ALONG MANIFOLD VALLEY

DISTANCE/TIME	5.9 miles (9.5km) / 3hrs 30min
ASCENT/GRADIENT	920ft (280m) / ▲ ▲
PATHS	Hard surface on Manifold Way, other footpaths can be rough in places and muddy in wet weather, many stiles
LANDSCAPE	Woodland, meadows and valleys
SUGGESTED MAP	OS Explorer OL24 Peak District – White Peak Area
START/FINISH	Grid reference: SK095561
DOG FRIENDLINESS	Keep on lead near livestock, under control at all other times; cattle may be present
PARKING	On Manifold Way near Wetton Mill
PUBLIC TOILETS	At Wetton Mill and beside village hall in Warslow
NOTES	Exercise extreme caution at footpath exit on to B5053 near Warslow

Described by one local as 'A line starting nowhere and ending up at the same place', the narrow gauge Leek and Manifold Valley Light Railway was one of England's most picturesque white elephants. Though it survived a mere 30 years from its first run in June 1904, its legacy is still enjoyed today. It ran for 8 miles (12.9km) from Hulme End to Waterhouses, where passengers and freight had to transfer to the standard-gauge Leek branch of the North Staffordshire Railway. The narrow-gauge railway owed its existence to Leek businessmen who feared that their town would lose out because of the newly opened Buxton-to-Ashbourne line.

Destined to fail

Engineer Everard Calthorp, who built the Barsi Railway near Mumbai, used the same techniques and design of locomotive for this line, and as a result it looked more like a miniature Indian railway than a classic English line. The potential success of the line was based on the supposition that the Ecton Copper Mines would re-open and that an extension to Buxton would tap into a lucrative tourist market. But the mines didn't re-open and the extension was never built. To survive, the small railway made a daily collection of milk from local farms and hauled produce from the creamery at Ecton for onward transportation to London. Passenger traffic was light, and when tourists did flock to the area on summer weekends it often caused severe overloading of the carriages. Even with this seasonal upturn the line never made a profit, and when the creamery shut in 1933 it was the end of the road for the miniature trains. The last one ran on 10 March 1934. The track was lifted and the bed presented by the railway company to Staffordshire County Council. They had the remarkable foresight to be one of the first local authorities to take a disued railway line and convert it into a pedestrian path.

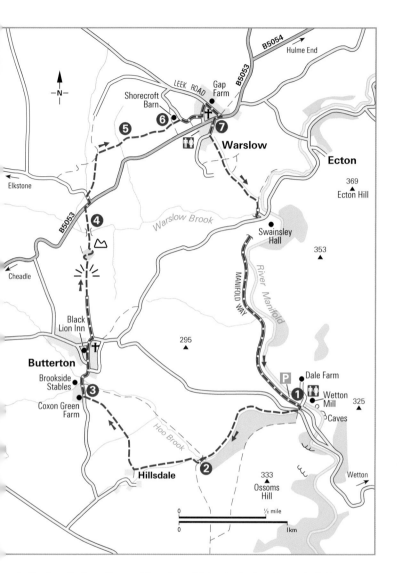

1. Head south down the road then turn right on to the lane towards Butterton. Almost immediately turn right (before the ford) and go through a gate on the left and walk along a valley-bottom track.

2. Two junctions with three footbridges come in quick succession. Follow signs to Hillsdale, going straight ahead then right. Cross a small ford, then bend left at the start of fields. Rise near the field edge, flanking a hill then climbing more steeply to Hillsdale. Turn right, following a footpath over several fields and stiles, aiming roughly for the spire at Butterton. Emerge on to the road opposite Coxon Green Farm.

3. Turn right along the road, cross the long ford and then head uphill. Higher up, fork right away from Pothooks Lane to go past the church and Black Lion Inn. Turn right at a T-junction on to Waste Lane, then go left on to a track at

a white flagpole. Cross a stile into fields, then head beside a row of trees and along a grassy spur. From a fingerpost, descend steeply on a rough and faint path through some trees and down to cross the stream via a shady wooden bridge.

4. Head directly uphill, away from the visible road embankment, then keep a hedge on your left. Cross a stile then exercise extreme caution as you exit directly on to a fast road on a slight but blind bend. Cross over, then fork almost immediately left towards Elkstone. Fork right across a stile on to a footpath, cross a couple of fields, then turn right behind a small derelict building. Follow the line of the wall, cross a stile then a stream and head uphill, keeping the fence on your left.

5. Towards the top of the field, just before the fence meets the wall at a large tree, cross a stile on the right. Head diagonally across the next field, veering left of a line of mature trees. Cross a stile and go through a gap in the next hedgerow. Cross to a gate at the far top corner of the next field, then across boggy ground. Fork diagonally across three small fields to a junction of paths at the next field corner (where a wall meets a hedge).

6. Go through a gate and ahead through the next field to emerge on the road by Shorecroft Barn. Turn right, then at the end, opposite the church, go left. When you reach the T-junction, turn right and pass Gap Farm.

7. At the T-junction with Cheadle Road, cross over on a dog-leg right then left on to School Lane. At a bend right, fork left through a squeeze stile on to a footpath. Descend gently through long narrow fields. Descend through scrub beside a wooded area, then zigzag over a stile and turn right to join the Manifold Way. Follow this easy, well-defined trail through an old railway tunnel, back to the car park.

Where to eat and drink

The Black Lion Inn in Butterton is a good place to relax for an evening after a day's walking (closed on Mondays). Built in 1782, this atmospheric, country hostelry has low beams, roaring open fires and a choice of real ales. Wetton Mill Tea Rooms offers hot and cold drinks, ice creams and snacks.

What to see

The walk passes through a tunnel that served the old railway. This is close to Swainsley Hall, which was the home of the Wardle family at the time of construction. They were shareholders in the company building the railway line, and although happy to take any profits going, they did not want to be troubled by seeing the trains from their house.

While you're there

Visit the old station at Hulme End. Now the Manifold Valley Visitor Centre, it has excellent displays covering the history of the Leek and Manifold Valley Light Railway and the industries and communities it served. There is also a scale model of the line with Hulme End Station as it was in its heyday.

FROM GRINDON TO THOR'S CAVE

DISTANCE/TIME	4.8 miles (7.7km) / 3hrs 30min
ASCENT/GRADIENT	1,020ft (311m) / ▲ ▲
PATHS	Field paths, some narrow and muddy, hard trail, limestone – may be slippery, several stiles
LANDSCAPE	Hillside, valley, meadows and woodland
SUGGESTED MAP	OS Explorer OL24 Peak District – White Peak Area
START/FINISH	Grid reference: SK084545
DOG FRIENDLINESS	Keep on short lead near livestock and on Manifold Track to prevent tripping other users; under close control at all other times
PARKING	At Grindon church
PUBLIC TOILETS	None on route

Set within the Manifold Valley, whose river rises within a mile of the Dove on Axe Edge, Thor's Cave may be recognisable to you if you've seen Ken Russell's horror film *The Lair of the White Worm* (1988). The opening shot of the film features the famous landmark, and you may, as a result, feel slightly apprehensive when climbing the path up the hillside.

Evidence of the past

The River Manifold heads south through superb limestone country, twisting and turning and passing some amazing geological features. These include the copper-rich Ecton Hill, the spoils of which made the 5th Duke of Devonshire enough money to build the fashionable and elegant Crescent at Buxton in the 18th century, as well as bustling Beeston Tor.

The awesome Thor's Cave, a gaping void in a 300 ft (91m) crag, was the home of prehistoric life forms. Along with nearby Ossom's and Elderbush Caves, it has been excavated and revealed bones and flints from the Stone and Bronze Ages. Formed over thousands of years from the combined effects of wind and rain on the soft limestone, it probably sheltered animals like giant red deer and bears, as well as early humans. Excavations have revealed a Bronze Age burial site, although much of the evidence was lost by somewhat over-zealous 19th-century excavators.

All Saints

The elegant spire of All Saints church in Grindon is visible from around the valley, earning it the nickname the Cathedral of the Moorlands. The present building is from 1848 but the first church was built in the 11th century as a chapel of ease for St Bartram in Ilam. The War Memorial tablet inside the church shows those of the village who fought in World War I.

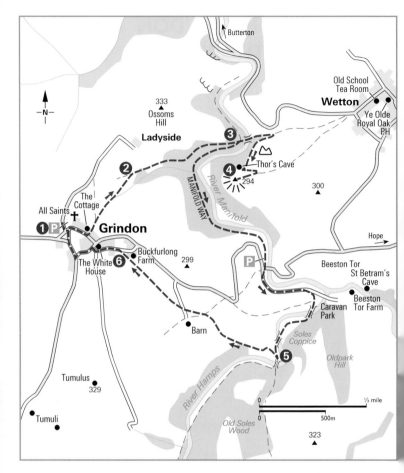

1. From the car park turn left then head downhill past the play area. Immediately past The Cottage fork left on to a track and go through a squeeze stile. Cross a field and head downhill, keeping to the right of two diverging paths. Cross a bridge, go through a gate and head downhill, with the stream and the wood on your right.

2. At the wall at the far end go through a gap stile on your right, continuing downhill into National Trust land at Ladyside. A narrow path runs by a fence into woodland. At a gate fork right and down a field edge then back into scrubbier woodland, descending steeply to a stile by the Manifold Way.

3. Cross the multi-use track, then a bridge, and take the path uphill following the signs for Thor's Cave. Immediately approaching the mouth of the cave, turn left. Continue on a track uphill, curve right before a gate and follow the path to the summit for superb views along the Manifold Valley.

4. Retrace your steps to the Manifold Way and turn left. Continue past a car park, then across a road by a bridge. Of two tarmac tracks, take the far right one ahead (no motor vehicles), and eventually cross two bridges.

5. Immediately before the third bridge, fork right, back on yourself, and cross a stile towards Grindon. Follow the path back, parallel to the road and then curving left and uphill. Go through a gate, then follow the path uphill above a slight valley. Pass through a second gate by a dry dewpond, with a bramble-shrouded wall to your right. Continue rising straight ahead through successive rough pasture fields, passing a barn some distance to the left.

6. Head diagonally left of a farm through a couple of fields. Fork left on to the farm road, which becomes a walled path by a barn. Fork right to join a tarmac track which starts at The White House. Turn right on to the road, then almost immediately take the first left. Follow this road back to the church then turn right for the car park.

Where to eat and drink
From the summit slope of Thor's Cave, a footpath runs eastwards across the fields for just under a mile (1.6km) to Wetton. The Old School Tea Room is open limited hours (mostly weekends) but is a quirky and excellent café. Alternatively, Ye Olde Royal Oak is a 400-year-old pub located in the centre of the village and has long been popular with walkers. If the weather is fine, you can sit outside in the beer garden.

What to see
Near the church gates in Grindon is an old stone known as the Rindle Stone. It contains the inscription 'The lord of the manor of Grindon established his right to this Rindle at Staffordshire Assizes on March 17th 1862'. A rindle is a brook that only flows in wet weather. Why anyone would want to establish legal right to such a thing is not explained on the stone.

While you're there
The Canopy Walk at RSPB Coombs Valley (5 miles/8km) to the west is a short but pleasant addition to a lovely rugged nature reserve. Take food and drink for a picnic, though, as there isn't a café.

THE TISSINGTON TRAIL

DISTANCE/TIME	4.5 miles (7.2km) / 2hrs 30min
ASCENT/GRADIENT	705ft (215m) / ▲ ▲
PATHS	Field paths, lanes and an old railway trackbed, many stiles
LANDSCAPE	Village and rolling farm pastures
SUGGESTED MAP	OS Explorer OL24 Peak District – White Peak Area
START/FINISH	Grid reference: SK177520
DOG FRIENDLINESS	Mostly on farmland, keep dogs on lead and under control; avoid long stretchy leads on trail to avoid tripping other users
PARKING	Tissington Trail pay car park
PUBLIC TOILETS	At car park

The approach to Tissington is through a magnificent avenue of lime trees, and when you first see the place it completes the idyll of a perfect village. On one side of a huge green is Tissington Hall, the home of the Fitzherbert family since the reign of Elizabeth I; on the other a neat row of cottages and a slightly elevated Norman church. The trouble with Tissington is that it is too perfect, and to avoid the crowds you'll have to visit mid-week. On this walk you save Tissington village for last, preferring instead to take to the Tissington Trail, the former trackbed of the Ashbourne-to-Buxton railway, which was closed by Dr Beeching in 1967. The route soon leaves the old track behind and descends into the valley of Bletch Brook, then out again on to a pastured hillside. Now you see Parwich, tucked in the next valley beneath a wooded hill. Overlooking the village is a fine 18th-century, red-brick building, Parwich Hall.

Parwich isn't as grand as Tissington, but it has a village green, and there's a duck pond too. You may see moorhens and their young swimming about among the tangled irises. But Parwich is a more peaceful place and the winding lanes are almost traffic-free in comparison. St Peter's Church is Victorian, but incorporates the chancel arch and a carved tympanum from the old Norman church.

Leaving Parwich behind, the path continues over the hillside, back into the valley of Bletch Brook and the Tissington Trail, then back for a better look at Tissington. The village is known for its five wells, dotted along Chapel Lane, though note at least one (Coffin Well) is up a private driveway. Every year on Ascension Day Tissington's locals dress these wells. This involves making a clay-covered dressing frame on to which pictures are traced. Flower petals are then pressed into the clay, creating the elaborate patterns and pictures you see. The ceremony is unique to Derbyshire and the Peak District. Originally a pagan ceremony to appease the gods into keeping pure water flowing, it was later adopted by the Christian religion. During the Black Death, when people from neighbouring villages were being ravaged by the plague, the Tissington villagers were kept in good health, due, they believe, to the pure water from the five wells. At the base of the village there's a fine duck pond, complete with a handful of ever-hungry ducks, but most eyes will be on the magnificent Jacobean hall. If it's closed to visitors, you can view it through the fine wrought-iron gates built by Robert Bakewell, or get an elevated view from the churchyard.

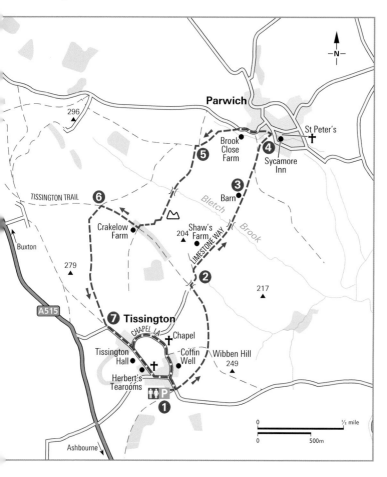

1. From the Tissington Trail car park follow the trail northbound along the trackbed of the former Ashbourne-to-Buxton railway. Take the second footpath on the left – by Trail Barn, signposted to Tissington and Parwich. This crosses the trail heading to the right over a bridge and along a cart track towards Shaw's Farm.

2. Cross a cattle grid on the first bend, then descend across fields on the waymarked but trackless path into the valley of Bletch Brook. Cross two stiles at the field boundaries and over a footbridge spanning the brook itself. A more definite path establishes itself on the climb out of the valley, passing under power lines, then across a sleeper bridge stile.

3. Follow the left field edge through two fields then squeeze through a stile. Descend a field towards the left edge of Parwich then bend briefly right along the next (short) field edge. Cross another stile, then descend a shady path to the village, emerging in view of the church.

4. At a path junction, turn right to explore the village. Otherwise go left following a path beside a small brook. Turn left on to a lane and head out of the village. Immediately past Brook Close Farm's driveway take a footpath left, roughly contouring across pasture. Bend left and uphill near the field edge, through a gate, then diagonally left across the next field. Cross a gate and a squeeze stile, then follow a sometimes muddy, tree-lined, short track ahead.

5. On entering the next field turn left. Follow the hedge on the left, then, veering half-right at the signpost, descend to recross Bletch Brook via two footbridges. Climb up the middle of the next long field before zigzagging up the steep upper slopes and then bending right to reach the bridge over the Tissington Trail. A long access path heads left before the bridge and down to the trail. Now follow the trail right past the Crakelow cutting.

6. After about 500yds (457m) take a footpath left towards Tissington. Go over a stile and cross to the right-hand corner of a field. Now follow a green lane, all the way down to the road at the edge of Tissington village.

7. Turn left along the lane to reach Chapel Lane. Explore the village, then take a left turn at either the T-junction at the bottom of The Foot or below the tea rooms, on to the road at the south of the village. Rise up round a bend to the right then fork right into the car park.

Where to eat and drink

Herbert's Tearooms at Tissington is licensed and serves lunch and afternoon teas. With its substantial outdoor seating area and good food, it's justifiably popular with walkers, cyclists and visitors to Tissington. The Sycamore Inn in Parwich is a good option for a mid-walk stop. It serves good bar meals and also incorporates the village shop.

What to see

Many of the regularly ploughed fields of Parwich and Tissington will have few wild flowers in them, but take a look at the field edges and the hayfields, for they will be rich in limestone-loving plants. In April and May, keep a watch for the increasingly rare cowslip (*Primula veris*). Its short single stem grows from a rosette of wrinkled leaves and its yellow flowers form a drooping cluster.

While you're there

Tissington Hall has been home to the Fitzherbert family for more than of 400 years, built by Francis Fitzherbert in 1609 to replace a moated manor house. Public tours on selected dates April to August.

DOVEDALE AND HALL DALE

DISTANCE/TIME	5.4 miles (8.7km) / 3hrs 30min
ASCENT/GRADIENT	1050ft (320m) / ▲▲
PATHS	Good paths, lanes, fields, polished limestone, one rough rocky eroded section, some stiles including tall stile on alternative route
LANDSCAPE	Partially wooded dales and high pastures, caves
SUGGESTED MAP	OS Explorer OL24 Peak District – White Peak Area
START/FINISH	Grid reference: SK146509
DOG FRIENDLINESS	Dogs should be kept on lead
PARKING	Dovedale pay car park, between Ilam and Thorpe
PUBLIC TOILETS	At car park (small charge) and Milldale
NOTES	Seasonal flooding risk: a section on Bunster Hill contains an eroded rough rocky section of bare polished limestone that can be slippery in dry weather and treacherous in wet conditions and is not recommended for inexperienced walkers (please follow the alternative route)

There's drama from the start as you follow the River Dove, travelling through a narrow gorge between Bunster Hill and the towering Thorpe Cloud. There are stepping stones to cross, then a limestone path climbs to a bold rocky outcrop above the river. Lovers' Leap has a fine view across the dale to the Twelve Apostles. In keeping with the name, in 1761 an Irish dean and his lady companion, who were out horse-riding, fell off the rock. The dean died of his injuries, but the lady survived to tell the tale.

The Dove writhes round another corner. Above your head, fingers of limestone known as the Tissington Spires rise out from thick woodland cover. On the right there's a splendid natural arch, which is just outside the entrance to the historic Reynard's Cave. The dale's limestone walls close in as boardwalk eases the way by the rushing river. As the valley opens out again two gigantic rock stacks face each other across the Dove. Pickering Tor has a small cave at its foot. A little footbridge allows you across to the other side to the foot of Ilam Rock. This 80ft (24m) leaning thumb of limestone has an overhang on the south side that's popular with climbers. It also has a cave at the bottom, which is only 6ft (2m) at the entrance, but opens out to over 30ft (9m) inside. You will get a better view of them when you cross the little footbridge to the cave at the foot of the rocks. On this side you're in Staffordshire and the paths are generally less populated. The continuing walk into Hall Dale heralds a less formal landscape. The dry dale climbs up the hillside past ancient woodland called Hurts Wood. Soon you're walking down a quiet lane with Ilam and the Manifold Valley on your right and Bunster Hill on your left. A path takes you across the shoulder of the hill, across the ridge and furrow of a medieval field system, then back into the valley of the Dove.

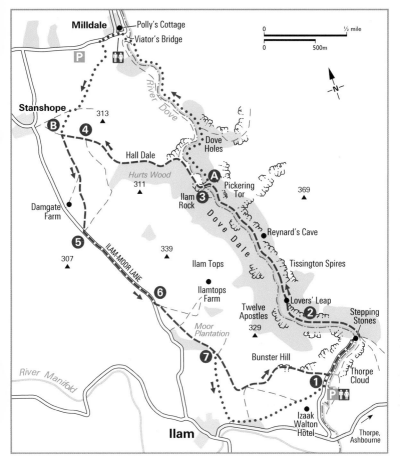

1. Take the dead-end lane up the west bank of the River Dove. Cross the stepping stones then turn left along the wide footpath which wanders through the pretty wooded dale between steep-sided limestone crags.

2. The path climbs some steps up to Lovers' Leap, then descends past Tissington Spires and Reynard's Cave. The dale narrows over boardwalk and past a cave, before rising slightly over a short, polished limestone section.

3. The dale widens again. Leave the main track for a path to Stanshope, crossing the Ilam Rock footbridge and following a narrow woodland path on the far bank. Ignore a path junction ('Ilam, steep ascent') after 200yds (183m). Cross a stile then bend left into Hall Dale, following the dry valley bottom up out of the woods into a rugged limestone-cragged gorge.

4. As the gorge becomes shallower, you enter pastureland with the attractive village of Stanshope now on the skyline. Ignore a path to the left by a stile then take the next path left (at Point B). Cross one field heading due south then follow a wall as it bends to the right in the next. At a shady tree, at the start of the next field, veer diagonally left and uphill. Go straight ahead in the next field for 50yds (46m) then diagonally right across a third to a country lane.

5. Turn left to walk along the lovely quiet lane (Ilam-Moor Lane), enjoying magnificent views across the Manifold Valley down to the right and towards Bunster Hill ahead.

6. After roughly 800yds (732m) and immediately before a farm drive entrance (Ilamtops Farm) cross a stile. Head across the drive to a second stile, then veer gently right from the drive and fractionally downhill over grassy pasture to the top of Moor Plantation woodlands. Cross a stile into access land and continue descending across the next field.

7. The main route (too experienced walkers only) contours across the hillside over a challenging section and through a notch in the hillside before descending steeply to the edge of access land above pasture. Head left and follow the wall line, eventually emerging onto the Dovedale Lane opposite the gauging station. Turn right to return to the car park.

The alternative route: One field beyond the end of Moor Plantation woods, fork right and down into a shallow grassy valley. Cross a tall stile on to a farm track, then turn left at a junction by a house. The track runs above a lane, skirting beneath Bunster Hill. Head uphill along the edge of access land, bending right with the line of the wall to the Dovedale Lane and car park.

Extending the walk As so often when walking beside the River Dove, it's difficult to resist the temptation to carry on following its lovely series of dales. You can do this at Point A, continuing up the dale to Viator's Bridge, a packhorse bridge in lovely Milldale. Head uphill from Milldale on a country lane, taking a footpath on the left after roughly 150yds (145m). After a few paces, fork right on a narrow path through thin woodland, then head across hilly fields towards Stanshope. Take a cart track heading right at the top of the hill, then a very easily missed footpath left back into fields to rejoin the main route at Point B.

Where to eat and drink
Polly's Cottage (takeaway kiosk) is on the walk extension in Milldale, and another kiosk operates in the Dovedale car park. For sit-down refreshments, the Izaak Walton Hotel can be accessed near the car park.

What to see
The Dove is a clear, pure river with brown trout and grayling feeding on caddisflies and mayflies. You may also see kingfishers diving.

While you're there
To enjoy the views from Thorpe Cloud, leave the main route at Dovedale's meeting with Lin Dale, then veer right from Lin Dale up the very steep grassy north flank to the summit.

ILAM AND THE RIVER MANIFOLD

DISTANCE/TIME	5.2 miles (8.4km) / 2hrs 45min
ASCENT/GRADIENT	820ft (250m) / ▲ ▲
PATHS	Tarmac roads, parkland, open hillside and shady woodland (may be muddy), many stiles
LANDSCAPE	Parkland, woodland and hillside
SUGGESTED MAP	OS Explorer OL24 Peak District – White Peak Area
START/FINISH	Grid reference: SK131507
DOG FRIENDLINESS	Keep on lead unless threatened by cattle
PARKING	At Ilam Hall National Trust pay car park
PUBLIC TOILETS	At Ilam Hall

The Manifold and Dove Rivers were both fished by Izaak Walton, known as the 'Father of Angling', and the author of *The Compleat Angler, or The Contemplative Man's Recreation*. Since the first edition appeared in 1653 it has never been out of print. Born in Stafford in 1593, Izaak Walton moved to London as an apprentice ironmonger, becoming a craftsman and guild member when he was 25 years old. For most of his working life he owned an ironmongers shop in Fleet Street and lived in a house in Chancery Lane. A keen angler, he spent much of his spare time fishing on the Thames, but it was not until retirement that he was able to devote himself to his hobby completely. 'I have laid aside business, and gone a-fishing.'

Shrewd operator

The view we have of Walton from his book is of a genial older man strolling along river banks in pastoral England. But nothing could be further from the truth. Walton lived during a period of political upheaval and unrest. In 1649 he saw the execution of Charles I and left London for Staffordshire, where he stayed during the Civil War. A staunch Royalist, he is mentioned among the supporters of Charles II after the Battle of Worcester in 1651. Following the battle he visited a friend who had been imprisoned in Stafford. From this friend Walton received the king's ring, which he delivered to Colonel Blague, then a prisoner in the Tower of London. The colonel escaped, made his way to France and returned the ring to the king. If Walton had been caught, he would have been executed. Just two years after 'the only known adventure' in his life he published his famous book.

The Compleat Angler is the story of three sportsmen – Viator, a huntsman, Auceps, a fowler, and Piscator, the fisherman – who walk the River Lea on May Day, debating the finer points of their sport. The fifth edition in 1676 contained an addition by Walton's friend, Charles Cotton, who lived at Beresford Hall near Hartington. Cotton built a fishing house on the banks of the Dove near his home, which still stands today. This 'holy shrine for all anglers' has the interlacing initials of both men and the inscription 'Piscatoribus Scarum 1674'.

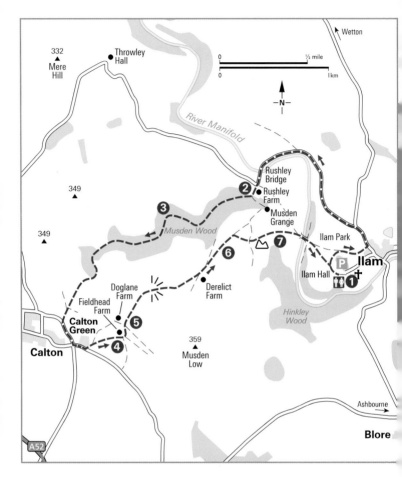

1. Leave the car park from the corner by the information panel (pedestrian exit) and turn right through a black iron gate. Follow the 'Circular Walk' on a faint track through the park around to the right. Cross a stile and turn left on to the road out of Ilam village. Go uphill, then turn left on to the Castern and Throwley Road. Fork left with the road towards The Orchards, then across Rushley Bridge.

2. Go through Rushley Farm, then turn right through an easily missed walkers' gate. It's beside sheep pens and before the drive up to Musden Grange. A second gate leads into hilly pasture. Bend left into a valley bottom, continuing through woodland then several fields.

3. Go over a series of stiles and gates and, at the final one, turn left on to a country lane. At the crossroads turn left towards Ashbourne. Go left through a gate at the next public footpath sign, and cross the field diagonally to a double stile. Maintain your direction diagonally across six fields, passing just to the left of a farm and crossing a tall and wide stile through a holly hedge.

4. At a gate in the hedge to the right of Fieldhead Farm turn left on to the gravel track. Follow this round the boundary of the farm then, at the second

bend left, take the easily missed second footpath on the right (just to the right of a metal gate).

5. Follow the field-edge path uphill. In the next field, pass a small depression in the ground then follow the left wall down the field. Join a farm road, pass a derelict farmstead, then veer right of the track. Head beside the field wall then through a gap stile in the far corner.

6. Follow the direction pointer past a redundant gap stile to a fallen down way-marker where fields to your right come to a corner at a tumbledown section of wall. Go right and follow the new wall on your right at the top of a sloping field. Go through a collapsed gap and veer diagonally left downhill, aiming just to the left of the pointed hill (Thorpe Cloud) ahead. After crossing both a clear then a faint vehicle track, the path through the grass becomes clearer.

7. Go across two fields, a stile and then a bridge and into Ilam Park. Turn right on to a track then at a gate fork left and uphill on a broad track that crosses the grounds back to the car park. Note that where the track fades, you should stay left of an apparent waymarker – it's just an orienteering post.

Where to eat and drink

The National Trust's Manifold Tea Room, located above the shop and overlooking the terraced gardens of Ilam Hall, provides welcome refreshment. It's open at weekends throughout the year and daily in the summer. There is a large area of outside seating that allows terrific views across the park.

What to see

As you cross Ilam Park, try to pick out the well-preserved remains of medieval ridge and furrow fields on the right-hand side. Look for the track that runs across them. It was once used by local tradesmen and servants at Ilam Hall who were forbidden to use the main drive.

While you're there

In the grounds of the hall, kids (of all ages) can enjoy a game of Pooh Sticks on St Bertram's Bridge then continue on to the 'natural play' area of Hinkley Hollow, where den building and log balancing are encouraged. Alternatively, try the family-friendly orienteering course. Those wishing for more sedate entertainment may enjoy visiting the ruins of Throwley Old Hall, the imposing remnants of a former medieval manor house standing proud above the Manifold Valley.

45

AROUND CARSINGTON AND BRASSINGTON

DISTANCE/TIME	6.3 miles (10.1km) / 3hrs 30min
ASCENT/GRADIENT	870ft (265m) / ▲ ▲
PATHS	Hilly field paths, some hard to follow, and railway trackbed, many stiles
LANDSCAPE	Limestone hills
SUGGESTED MAP	OS Explorer OL24 Peak District – White Peak Area
START/FINISH	Grid reference: SK249528
DOG FRIENDLINESS	Dogs on lead over farmland, under close control everywhere else; avoid long stretchy leads on High Peak Trail to avoid tripping other users
PARKING	Sheepwash pay car park by Carsington Water
PUBLIC TOILETS	None on route

'He was as lean as a Skeleton, pale as a dead corpse, his hair and beard a deep black, his flesh lank, and, as we thought, something of the colour of lead itself.' So wrote Daniel Defoe on seeing a lead miner, who had been living in a cave at Harboro Rocks. In times past Carsington and Brassington lived and breathed lead. Prior to the construction of Carsington Water archaeologists discovered a Romano-British settlement here, which could have been the long-lost Ludutarum, the centre of the lead-mining industry in Roman times. As you walk out of Carsington into the world of the miner, you're using the very tracks he would have used. But the lesions and pockmarks of the endless excavations are being slowly healed by time, and many wild flowers are beginning to proliferate in the meadows and on hillsides.

Weird-shaped limestone crags top the hill, then Brassington appears in the next valley with its Norman church tower rising above the grey rooftops of its 17th- and 18th-century houses. Brassington's former post office used to be the tollhouse for the Loughborough turnpike. St James Church is largely Norman, though it was heavily restored in the late 19th century, including the north aisle, which was added in 1880. High on the inner walls of the Norman tower is a figure of a man with his hand on his heart. The carving is believed to be Saxon: the man, Brassington's oldest resident.

Climbing out of Brassington the route takes you over Hipley Hill, where there are more remnants of the mines, and more limestone outcrops. On the top you could have caught the train back, but the Cromford High Peak Railway closed in 1967, so you are left with a walk along its trackbed. It's a pleasant walk though, through a wooded cutting, with meadow cranesbill and herb Robert thriving among trackside verges and crags. Harboro Rocks beckon from the left. Archaeologists have uncovered evidence that sabre-toothed tigers, black bears and hyenas once sought the shelter of nearby caves. They also discovered relics and artefacts from Roman and Iron Age dwellers.

For those with extra time, there's an path winding between the popular climbing crags to the summit, which gives wide views across the White Peak and the lowlands of the East Midlands. There are perfect views of Carsington Water and its surrounds. Leaving the railway behind, there's one last hill, Carsington Pasture, to descend before returning to the lake.

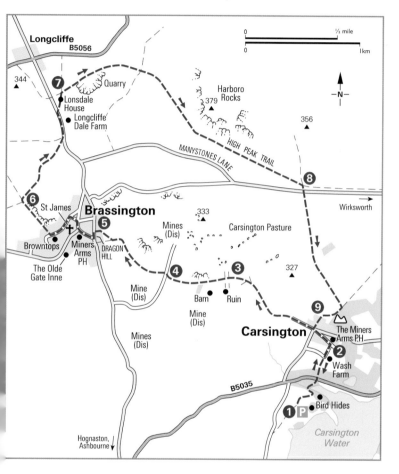

1. Take the 'Carsington Water Circular Route' path northwards. Passing two bird hide paths, it winds through scrub woods and rounds a finger of the lake before crossing the B5035 road. Continue up the far side, meeting a lane by Wash Farm then entering the village by The Miners Arms.

2. Head left through the village to a sharp bend left. Now go straight ahead along a narrow lane passing several cottages. Beyond a gate the lane becomes a fine green track beneath the limestone-studded slopes of Carsington Pasture.

3. The track swings left to a gate below some wind turbines; immediately beyond the gate take the narrower right fork off the main path. This climbs up grassy slopes with numerous other tracks criss-crossing the high rough

pasture. Towards a small copse, go past a redundant stone squeeze stile, pass right of the copse and through a former gateway in a tumbledown wall. Now descend a green track into a little valley, crossing one more field to a green lane.

4. Cross over this, following a miners' track up to some old workings. As the track bends sharp right, fork left on to a narrower track with Brassington soon in view ahead. Cross a stile then follow a wall on your left to the next stile. Turn left, then part-way down the next field, fork diagonally right across fields to a track at the edge of the village.

5. At Smithy Barn turn left on to Dragon Hill, then immediately right up a road to the Miners Arms pub. Turn right on to a side road directly opposite the pub, then sharp left up Red Lion Hill. Turn left again at the T-junction, continuing above the church. Opposite Browntop, fork right on to a footpath which climbs diagonally past more mining holes and spoil heaps.

6. Cross the head of a green lane then take the right of two trackless footpaths (Limestone Way). The path crosses under a line of wooden electricity pylons. In the third field, bear half-right above the small rock outcrops – the way is vague here. Now aim for the extensive buildings of Longcliffe Dale Farm, turning left at the road. Past the farm, a footpath on the right then cuts a corner to the High Peak Trail. This passes an electricity substation and a stables, bending right at the stables' gates and down a short grassy track to the High Peak Trail.

7. Turn right along the trackbed of the High Peak Trail, passing Harboro Rocks.

8. Drawing level with two groups of wind turbines, turn right and across a small field on a footpath to Carsington. Cross a road, then follow the wall across Carsington Pasture. Approaching woodland, descend steeply to a gate by a cottage.

9. Turn left down a little stepped alley, which broadens to become Mining Lane. Fork left as it joins the road back to The Miners Arms. Now retrace your earlier route back to Sheepwash car park.

Where to eat and drink

You can break the route for refreshment in Brassington – both Miners Arms and The Olde Gate Inne are pleasant pubs which serve food as well as drinks. Towards the end of the walk, The Miners Arms in Carsington has a lovely outdoor seating area and the food is good.

What to see

Despite their apparently sterile soil, the spoil tips have been colonised by a range of lead-tolerant plants, flourishing among the grassy heaps. You may see mountain pansy, spring sandwort, eyebright or autumn gentians.

While you're there

Why not hire a bike at Carsington Water (main car park)? The gravel track around the reservoir, much of which is at the water's edge, is perfect for leisure cycling whatever your age. See if you can find the secret wooden house on the far side, not far from Millfields car park. Alternatively there are family-friendly short tracks around Stone Island.

46

FROM AMBERGATE TO CRICH

DISTANCE/TIME	7.5 miles (12.1km) / 3hrs 30min
ASCENT/GRADIENT	950ft (290m) / ▲ ▲ ▲
PATHS	Short section of busy roadside pavement at start/end, woodland and field paths and canal towpath, a couple of narrow road sections with no pavement, some stiles
LANDSCAPE	Woods and pastured hills, quarried edges
SUGGESTED MAP	OS Explorer OL24 Peak District – White Peak Area
START/FINISH	Grid reference: SK349515
DOG FRIENDLINESS	Keep on lead – and keep out of the canal to protect water voles and other wildlife
PARKING	Ambergate pay car park by station
PUBLIC TOILETS	Near Sherwood Foresters Monument and in Crich

The first five minutes of the walk are somewhat uneventful and everyday but as soon as you turn the corner and cross over Poyser's Bridge you're walking in a different world, separate from the road and the railway. The canal, tangled with irises and pondweed, ambles by slowly through the trees. Watch out for the bright yellow-and-black spotted longhorn beetle feeding on the meadowsweet and the holly blue butterflies in springtime.

On this journey you save the greater part of the canal walking to the end, in order to climb through the woodland of Crich Chase, once part of a hunting forest owned by the 13th-century Norman baron Hubert FitzRalph. After climbing high fields and along a gritstone edge, known as The Tors, you come upon Crich (pronounced so the 'i' rhymes with eye). Older readers may get that déjà vu feeling – Crich was the setting for Cardale in *Peak Practice*, a popular 1990s TV drama featuring a country medical practice, after which the village chippy is still named. Beyond the market cross and over more fields you come to the Crich Tramway Village museum, which is well worth a visit.

The walk continues to its high point on Crich Stand, a limestone crag uplifted within an area of sandstone and gritstone. Capping the Stand is a 60ft (18m) beacon tower, rebuilt in 1922 to commemorate the Sherwood Foresters killed in World War I. On a clear day it is said you can see as far as the Humber Bridge. Often you'll see kestrels hovering around the cliff edge, searching for their prey. The path descends through more woodland, beneath the shady gritstone cliffs of the old Duke's Quarries and down to the canal at Whatstandwell.

The canal here has been allowed to silt up and has become a haven for wildlife, including endangered water voles. It's well known for its many varieties of hoverfly, its azure damselflies and brown china-mark moths.

Yellow irises and flowering rushes, which have pink flowers, can be seen at the water's edge, while dense green pondweed clogs the middle of the canal. That doesn't seem to impede the moorhens or mallards, though, and by the time you get back to Ambergate you will have seen a wealth of wildlife.

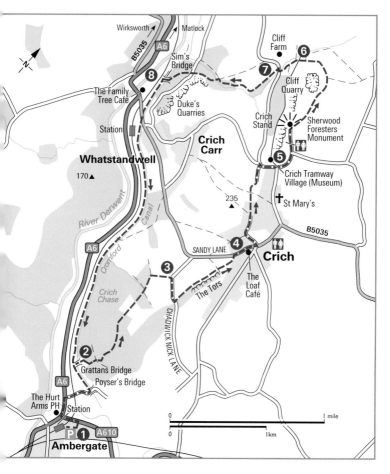

1. Walk down to the main road from the car park. Go left beneath the bridge and then right along the busy A6. Turn right up Chase Road, and underneath the railway bridge to the Cromford Canal at Poyser's Bridge. Follow the towpath left to Grattans Bridge.

2. Bend around left and over the bridge, then almost immediately take a gate on the left by a spring. A waymarked path winds up through the woodland of Crich Chase, steep at first, then almost contouring through occasional small clearings. Join a track, heading left to a field wall corner at the top of the woodland. Continue ahead between the treeline and the field fence. By the end of a crumbling wall, turn right over a stile, then rise up field edges to reach Chadwick Nick Lane.

3. Turn right along the road. At a fingerpost just beyond the brow of the hill, double back left up steps to a stile. Head north at the edge of successive fields with stiles, following the crest of The Tors ridge. Enter an enclosed path towards the far end, which descends gently to a road, emerging opposite Crich Fire Station.

4. Pass The Jubilee trees, then along a narrow section of road and down to the Market Place in Crich. Fork left up an unnamed road, then right up Coasthill, climbing ahead to its dead end. Follow a path ahead across a couple of fields, then fork right to join a track by a house and out to the road. Turn right and pass the Crich Tramway Village.

5. At a sharp right-hand bend, turn left towards the Memorial Tower. Take a footpath avoiding the road then go up the approach road to Crich Stand. Bear right below the monument on a stony footpath which eventually descends and curves left to skirt Cliff Quarry.

6. Cross the museum's tram track near its terminus and bear right on a descending woodland path. Towards the bottom, this crosses over a quarry track at a dog-leg junction under power lines. Fork left on to a small camp-site's driveway (Cliff Farm), then keep ahead to emerge on to a road.

7. Cross diagonally right to a footpath. Descend gently at the left field edge, continuing through scrub and eventually into a long wooded valley. Pass some imposing craggy remnants of the former Duke's Quarries then cross over a lane. The track opposite leads down through further woodland, forking right to cross Sim's Bridge over the canal, just north of Whatstandwell. Turn left towards Ambergate and loop round to join the canal towpath.

8. Now follow a delightful towpath for 2 miles (3.2km) through the shade of tree boughs. At Poyser's Bridge you meet the outward route and retrace your steps back to the car park.

Where to eat and drink
The Hurt Arms at Ambergate is a family-friendly pub that serves food. Also try The Loaf Café in Crich. Further on, there's The Family Tree licensed café near the canal at Whatstandwell.

What to see
The sunken track leading up through the start of woodland in Crich Chase is a classic example of a holloway where centuries of walking have ground a path below the normal surface level. In Crich, near Coasthill, look out for a small bridge beside the road. This marks the line of George Stephenson's Clay Cross Company railway track to Cliff Quarry. At Crich Stand, if open, go up the Sherwood Foresters Monument (there's a small fee) for the views.

While you're there
Take time to visit the Crich Tramway Village, where you can travel all day on vintage trams from all over the world. There's a period townscape, including the Georgian facade of Derby's old Market Place, which was relocated in 1972 after the Derby building was damaged by fire.

47

BELPER AND BLACKBROOK

DISTANCE/TIME	5.6 miles (9km) / 3hrs
ASCENT/GRADIENT	790ft (241m) / ▲ ▲
PATHS	Good paths and tracks, could be muddy after periods of heavy rain, several stiles
LANDSCAPE	Urban start and finish, but mostly rolling farm pastures
SUGGESTED MAP	OS Explorer 259 Derby
START/FINISH	Grid reference: SK346481
DOG FRIENDLINESS	Dogs should be kept on lead through farmland, under close control elsewhere
PARKING	Belper River Gardens car park, off A6
PUBLIC TOILETS	At River Gardens car park

Before Jedediah Strutt came to Belper, it was a mere backwater of Derbyshire, and according to Dr Davies, writing in 1811, was 'backward in civility' and considered as the insignificant residence of a few 'uncivilised nailors'. The land around Belper was part of the Norman hunting grounds of Beaurepaire, which meant beautiful retreat. The land was first handed to Henri de Ferrières and the family ruled here until 1266, when Henry III handed it over to his son the Earl of Leicester, known as Edmund Crouchback.

Strutt's legacy

Jedediah Strutt had earlier partnered Richard Arkwright in the building of the world's first water-powered cotton mill, sited upriver at Cromford. The success of that project prompted him to build the South Mill here at Belper. By 1786 he had built the timber-framed North Mill. Jedediah died in 1797, but his three sons, William, George and Joseph, built on his successes. In 30 years there were five mills in the town, though the original North Mill had to be replaced in 1803 after a damaging fire. The Strutts took an active interest in the welfare of their community, providing good housing for their workforce and schooling for the children. As you walk past the North Mill you can see a bridge connecting it with the mill across the road. Note the gun loopholes in it. They were to protect the mills from Luddites, but fortunately the trouble never materialised.

Rural scenes

Most of the walk is rural, and you're soon tramping through woods and across fields. The small lake you see is now a nature reserve, known for its wildfowl. Farm tracks that wouldn't look out of place in a Gainsborough or Constable landscape take you up the hillside to Belper Lane End. At the top of the hill you reach Longwalls Lane, which was part of the Saxon Portway road. Archaeological finds show that the lane was in use, not only by the Romans, but by prehistoric man. In such times the ridges made safer routes than the swampy forests of the valleys, with their dangerous wild animals.

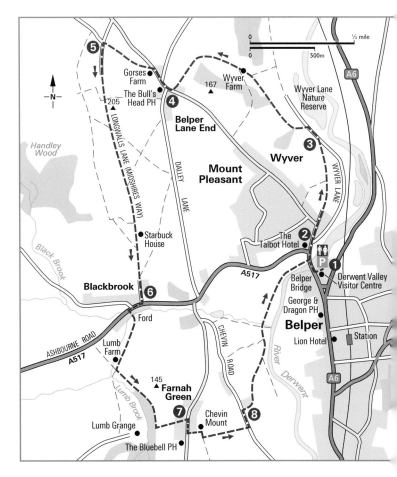

1. Exit the River Gardens car park by a pedestrian passageway near the public toilets. This leads past the back of the mills and the Derwent Valley Visitor Centre. Exit the driveway bearing right then over Belper Bridge. By The Talbot Hotel, turn right towards 'Belper Lane End Alderwasley'.

2. Ignore the next two right forks (Wyver Lane and Belper Lane), but where the road swings sharply left, go straight ahead on The Scotches. At the end of this short lane, a stile leads to a path across a field. Follow this at the edge of several more fields before descending through woodland to Wyver Lane, near the wetlands nature reserve.

3. Turn left along the road. Take a track bearing left signed to Wyver Farm; this bends right through a long field then becomes a green lane. Pass straight through the yard of Wyver Farm then continue through fields to the road at Belper Lane End.

4. Turn right along the road, then right again at the Bull's Head pub. Stay left with the main road towards Shottle, then turn left on to a farm track at Gorses Farm. Follow this uphill, continuing ahead when it becomes a narrow path by a barn.

5. Turn left along Longwalls Lane, which soon degenerates into a stony track. Any vehicle traffic is restricted beyond a sharp bend right of the main track. Continue ahead on a track which becomes rutted grass, then a narrower and rocky, tree-lined holloway. It becomes wider and open to traffic again at Starbuck House. Descend to a T-junction with the Ashbourne Road at Blackbrook.

6. Turn right along the road and pass Plains Lane. Take the next left on to a tarmac track. Cross a footbridge by a ford, then rise up the lane. Pass Lumb Farm and Windarra then take a footpath on the left. Past a gate, a path climbs diagonally across a field, then enters an area of delightful woodland (Lumb Grange). Turn left at a stile in a wall, aiming for some houses at the far end of a field. Take the right hand of two parallel tracks, past the houses to reach the road at Farnah Green.

7. Turn right along the road to walk past some houses. Shortly before The Bluebell pub, turn left on to a tarmac driveway to Chevin Mount. This becomes unsurfaced then bends sharp right. At a nearby bench, turn left down a fenced-in footpath, descending steeply and directly beside sloping fields to Chevin Road.

8. The continuing path is staggered 100yds (91m) to the left and follows a short driveway past Swiss Barn. Go through a walkers' gate then go left on a well-marked footpath. This leads across fields and down to the River Derwent. Stay near the river, crossing a driveway track on a dog-leg left then right, then along wider tracks back to Belper Bridge and the outward route.

Where to eat and drink
The Bull's Head at Belper Lane End has a large restaurant area, which serves food seven days a week and has a good range of ales and wines. Belper also has some good pubs, including The George & Dragon and the Lion Hotel on Bridge Street.

What to see
The Wyver Lane Nature Reserve is one of Derbyshire Wildlife Trust's most important wetland reserves. Although there is no access to the reserve itself there is a bird hide and the lane you walk up overlooks it. The reserve is home to otters as well as several bird species including tufted ducks, sandpipers and lapwings.

While you're there
In 2001 the Derwent Valley Mills area was designated a World Heritage Site by UNESCO for its industrial heritage. It's worth a visit to the Derwent Valley Visitor Centre at North Mill, whose iron frame was developed in response to mill fires. The centre has exhibitions illustrating the development of the region during the Industrial Revolution, including Hargreave's revolutionary spinning jenny, Arkwright's water frame and Crompton's mule, and offers several guided walks throughout the year on Belper and its fascinating history.

OSMASTON AND SHIRLEY PARKS

48

DISTANCE/TIME	4.8 miles (7.7km) / 2hrs 30min
ASCENT/GRADIENT	460ft (140m) / ▲
PATHS	Estate tracks and field paths, several stiles
LANDSCAPE	Park, woodland and farm pasture
SUGGESTED MAP	OS Explorer 259 Derby
START/FINISH	Grid reference: SK199435
DOG FRIENDLINESS	Dogs should be on lead
PARKING	Osmaston Village Hall car park on Moor Lane, next to school
PUBLIC TOILETS	None on route

Osmaston is barely a few winding country lanes away from the buzzing traffic of Ashbourne, but it's just the unspoiled tranquil village you'd hope to find on a country walk. The moment you leave the car you will experience the slow tickover of the place.

St Martin's Church was built in 1845 to replace a much earlier one. The parish register goes back to 1606. It's full of references to the Wright family, who for a long time were the local gentry and benefactors to the village. Francis Wright, the owner of the Butterley Iron Works, had Osmaston Manor built here in 1849. The hall itself was a mock-Tudor mansion and the gardens were landscaped. In 1964 the hall's owner, Sir John Walker, decided to demolish the place when he moved to Okeover and took the Okeover family name. However, Osmaston Manor is well served by public rights of way, which make a pleasing itinerary for the walker.

Across the road from the car park is a terrace of four thatched cottages, built to celebrate the coronation of King George VI. As you walk down the lane you pass The Shoulder of Mutton, a fine village pub with much promise for the end of the day (closed between 3pm–6pm), then some more of those thatched cottages, this time built with rustic local bricks. These cottages are much older than the ones seen earlier and they're timber framed. At the end of the lane there's a duck pond. The walk enters the woodlands of Osmaston Park and threads between two of the estate's many lakes. On the other side there's an old mill, built in the style of an Austrian chalet and complete with a waterwheel. The path climbs through more woodland.

Shirley is another pretty village with its own aristocracy: Earl Ferrers and the Shirley family. From Shirley the walk turns back across fields and woods to Osmaston Park, reaching another of the estate's lakes. This one has the best setting, with a lush meadow surround and the occasional heron.

As you continue along the track, heading north and back into the woods now, you'll see an unexpected tower which is all that remains of Osmaston Manor. The tower was designed to accommodate all the hall's various chimneys in one single stack. With this odd sight still lingering in your thoughts, the walk ends in fine 'lord of the manor' style as you walk down the manor's main drive, saluted by a grand avenue of lime trees.

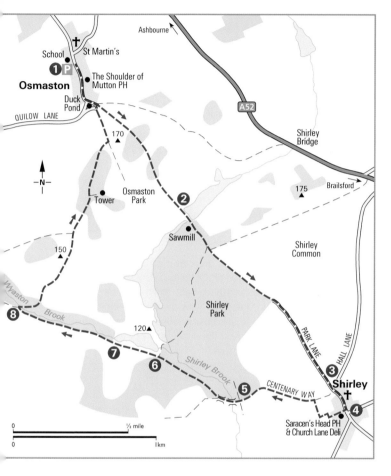

1. Turn right from the car park and follow the road past The Shoulder of Mutton pub to the village green and duck pond. Turn left and then take the middle of three rights of way. The gravel track rises slightly between fields and through attractive woodland. Descend past a farm to the left.

2. Pass between two elongated lakes, then beside an old water-powered sawmill. Stay on the track ahead, climbing up through mature woodlands and over a junction at the top, eventually gaining tarmac and descending towards Shirley.

3. Turn right at a T-junction, and descend to the Saracen's Head public house.

4. Immediately before the pub, turn right down a gravel track, bend right then fork left beside a red-brick building. Cross a stile into fields, then bend sharp right, following the field edge. At the start of the next field turn left and follow

Centenary Way markers along field edges. (You will bend right then cross a stile in the corner and turn right. Go diagonally right across the next field, then turn left). Now descend towards a wood, which is the southern extremity of Shirley Park.

5. Fork right off the track at a gateway and on to a narrower track through grass. Cross an estate track, then over duckboards, and a footbridge over Shirley Brook. Further duckboards lead to a fork right. Cross another footbridge then follow the path through the woods. There's a short bend left at a boggy section, then you join a rough brick-strewn track coming from a gateway to your left. Turn left at a track junction, then follow waymarkers ahead on the rough track. Look for a patch of mosaic tiling, possibly from the former hall.

6. Beyond a gate at the edge of the woods, ignore the Centenary Way path on the right. Instead, continue along a grassy vehicle track through the pasture ahead and alongside a pleasant lake, the southernmost of the Osmaston Park lakes.

7. Where the track bears diagonally left, continue ahead alongside the lake, then on a narrow track between old and new fences. You are walking through the Wyaston Brook Valley and, although the path is faint on the ground, the stiles in the cross-fences are all in place, if occasionally a tad rickety.

8. The bridleway from Wyaston Grove joins the route just beyond one of these stiles and is easily missed (grid ref SK195422). Double-back right along it, following some railings around to the right. Climb out of the valley and over a grassy hill. Just beyond the Tower View, this track becomes a tarmac drive. Turn left at two estate track junctions, then leave the estate on an avenue of lime trees. Emerge once more at the village green, pass the duck pond, then turn right to return to the car park.

Where to eat and drink
If you're after a traditional Sunday lunch, try The Shoulder of Mutton at Osmaston. The Saracen's Head at Shirley serves excellent food as a mid-walk stop, and the Church Lane Deli in its car park serves ethically sourced takeaway coffee, freshly baked cakes and Daltons ice cream.

What to see
The lakes are frequented by many birds, including grey heron, mallards, moorhens and many migratory wildfowl. In the woodlands look out for very tall, broad trunked pine trees. These are giant redwoods, more typically associated with the USA than the UK. The show of the Ashbourne Shire Horse Society is held in Osmaston Park in August.

While you're there
Ashbourne proclaims itself to be the gateway to Dovedale and has some fine old coaching inns and an interesting range of small shops.

MACKWORTH AND MARKEATON

DISTANCE/TIME	6.5 miles (10.5km) / 3hrs
ASCENT/GRADIENT	460ft (140m) / ▲
PATHS	Farm tracks and field paths, can be muddy after rain, several stiles
LANDSCAPE	Undulating fields, crops and pasture
SUGGESTED MAP	OS Explorer 259 Derby
START/FINISH	Grid reference: SK332379
DOG FRIENDLINESS	Dogs should be kept under close control and must not enter the playground in Markeaton Park
PARKING	Markeaton Park pay car park (signed from road as Mundy Play Centre)
PUBLIC TOILETS	At Markeaton Park

Markeaton Park's a bustling place in summer, but as soon as you cross the road and take the lane up to Markeaton Stones Farm you leave that all behind to enter a rural world. The farmhouse and stables are pristine, made from warm-red local brick. Beyond Markeaton Stones, the track wends its way between rolling arable fields that slope gently right to a stream, here called Markeaton Brook. Transformed into ribbon-like lakes, the brook provides a tranquil focus for the landscaped parks of Kedleston and Markeaton, before eventually joining the River Derwent.

As you climb the hill towards hilltop trees, look back and see Derby spread before you. Prominent in the view are the university, with its rooftop masts, and the cathedral, which dwarfs everything around it. The beeches of Vicar Wood guide you past the farm of the same name to the other side of the hill, where you can see mile upon mile of rolling farmland. Hidden behind the trees lie the landscaped parklands of Kedleston Hall. Famous Scottish architect Robert Adam, built the present hall for Nathaniel Curzon in 1759.

A short stretch of road leads to the entrance to Meynall Langley Gardens and their café. In the next cross-field section the walking is a little rougher, but it's still pleasantly pastoral despite the Derby skyline and a hilltop water tower providing an unexpectedly pleasing distant backdrop to rolling fields. As you reach the busy A52 there's a brief abrupt return to the present day, but Mackworth village is a surprise. A tidy row of 17th- and 18th-century cottages lines an undulating, slightly twisted lane. In the middle is a Gothic stone-built gatehouse, the remains of Mackworth Castle, which was built around 1495 for the de Mackworth family, and destroyed in the Civil War. At the end of the lane is the church of All Saints, a rather austere 14th-century building with a Perpendicular tower. The last mile of the route follows the Bonnie Prince Charlie Walk across fields and back to Markeaton Park.

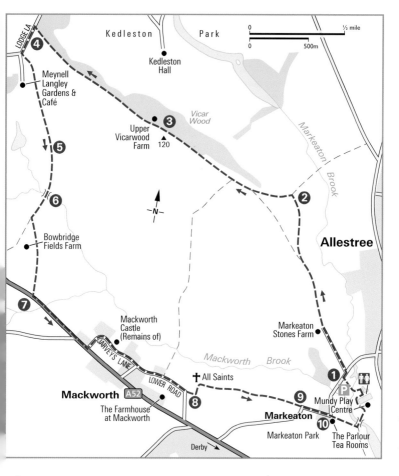

1. From the car park cross the road and head briefly right to gain a tarmac track to Markeaton Stones Farm. Past the farm, the track becomes stony and climbs gently around fields. At a fork, keep right until it reaches a junction.

2. Turn left here along a smooth tarmac track. Fork ahead where the main track bends to the left, now on rougher tarmac and climbing up to Upper Vicarwood Farm.

3. Keep an eye out for feathery-footed free-range cockerels as you cross the farmyard, then continue through a gate by the left-hand side of the stable block. Follow a hilltop track (which can become surprisingly boggy in sustained wet conditions); ignore a fork off to the left part-way along.

4. Turn left along a country lane. At a bend right (by the entrance to Meynell Langley Gardens), fork left through a field gate. Head down the right edge of fields, then enter a rough copse. Follow another field edge beyond, which leads into pasture.

5. Head across the centre of this widening field, in a rightwards-trending arc. Part-way down the field, a large ash tree becomes visible on the far boundary.

Aim for a gate just left of this. Cross the next field and over a wooden footbridge spanning Mackworth Brook.

6. The path now goes parallel to a hedge on the right, then through the field gate on the right at the far side. Bear left across the field corner to a former gateway, then continue across the upper edge of the next field. Pass a farm which hides behind trees to the right, then walk the length of an elongated field to the distant bottom-left corner by the road.

7. A kissing gate leads to a gap in a tall hedge and on to the pavement of the busy A52 (take care). Head to the left along this, passing a carwash and diner. Take the next left along Jarveys Lane, which becomes Lower Road and winds its way through Mackworth village.

8. Where the lane turns sharp right near the church, continue straight ahead on a footpath. Turn left into a field, heading just right of the church. Turn right by the graveyard; a well-defined path now leads beside several fields back to Markeaton.

9. Cross a road (which can be busy at rush hour) to find a pavement running leftwards behind vegetation. Pass the entrance to Bryers Heritage Farm and continue to a sharp bend left in the road.

10. Continue ahead through the gates into Markeaton Park. Swing left over bridges over two branches of Markeaton Brook, then left again to pass the Mundy Play Centre. At the far end of the play area, fork left over a red-painted bridge and up a few steps to return to the car park.

Where to eat and drink

Part-way around the walk, the café at Meynell Langley Gardens serves delicious cakes. Towards the end of the walk, there's The Parlour Tea Rooms on the corner of the road at Bryers Heritage Farm near Markeaton Park (closed Mondays and Tuesdays). For bar and restaurant meals try The Farmhouse at Mackworth.

What to see

Meynell Langley Gardens is a working nursery, producing the plants for sale. Modern glasshouses complement the old walled garden and orchards, where flowers, vegetables, fruit and ornamental trees are grown, while old and new varieties are compared in the trials garden, occasionally open under the National Garden Scheme.

While you're there

Kedleston Hall is worth seeing properly, once you've taken off your boots (May–October, check website for opening hours). Designed by Robert Adam, it's set in parklands with lakes, cascades and woodland. There's a marble hall, an Indian Museum with objects collected by Lord Curzon while he was Viceroy of India, and an exhibition of original Robert Adam drawings. Children, however, may well prefer the Mundy Play Centre (mostly free to use) and High Ropes Course (fee applies) near the car park at Markeaton Park.

50

TICKNALL AND CALKE ABBEY

DISTANCE/TIME	4.1 miles (6.6km) / 2hrs
ASCENT/GRADIENT	295ft (90m) / ▲
PATHS	Estate roads and field paths, a few stiles
LANDSCAPE	Parkland and crop fields
SUGGESTED MAP	OS Explorer 245 The National Forest
START/FINISH	Grid reference: SK352240
DOG FRIENDLINESS	On lead through farmland and abbey grounds
PARKING	Village Hall car park, off Ingleby Lane, Ticknall
PUBLIC TOILETS	At car park
NOTES	Entrance charge payable at Calke Abbey's Middle Lodge Gates

Calke is not an abbey at all. The Augustinian order of monks did build one here in 1133 and dedicated it to St Giles, but since 1622 it has been the family home of the Harpurs and Harpur-Crewes. In 1703 Sir John Harpur had the present Baroque mansion built on the site of the abbey, keeping some of the old 6ft (1.8m) walls. This was a high-society family, but things started to go wrong in the 1790s when Sir Henry Harpur took a lady's maid as his bride. Society shunned the couple and they, in turn, shunned society – the beginning of a tale of eccentricity and reclusiveness that would span two centuries.

Calke was a grand house with many rooms, and here was a family with money. When they tired of one room, they would just leave it the way it stood and move to another. For instance, when Sir Vauncey Harpur-Crewe married in 1876, he locked up his bachelor room, along with the heads of stuffed deer he had shot as a youth. When the National Trust acquired the house in 1985 they found a dust-laden, neglected, but intriguing place, filled with treasures of centuries gone by.

The tree-lined drive sets the scene. There's fallow deer in the woods, as well as barn and tawny owls. Betty's Pond is the first of the several lakes passed on the route. The house, being in a dip, hides until the last moment. Its magnificent three-storey south front includes a four-column Ionic portico. If it's open, it is well worth a visit to see, among others, the Gold Drawing Room and the 18th-century Chinese silk state bed.

Ticknall is an interesting village. Passing through it you see some pleasing timber-framed red-brick cottages. Near the abbey entrance driveway, you are confronted with a horseshoe-shaped bridge, arching over the road. Built in 1800, in a style typically used on canals, it was part of an old tramway system, which included a tunnel under the main drive to the abbey. Limestone from Ticknall's brickworks used to be carried by horse-drawn trams to the canal at Willesley. On the return journey the load would have been coal. The scheme was abandoned in 1915, and now just the bridge remains.

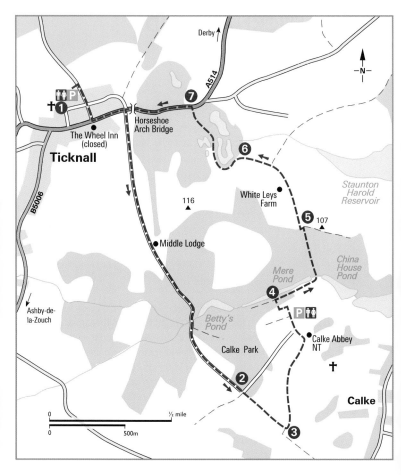

1. Turn right out of the car park and down to the main road. Turn left and then turn right to enter the Calke Abbey Estate. Go up a tarmac avenue lined with mature lime trees, then at the Middle Lodge Gates you will have to pay an entrance charge for the park and gardens. (There's an additional fee for the abbey itself, payable at the house.) Continue southeast along the road, passing Betty's Pond on your left.

2. Eventually the road turns sharply left at a crossing of paths; leave it here, continuing along a grassy track to the south end of the park.

3. Fork left by a white gate, doubling back towards the abbey which appears in a dip ahead. Turn left at the railings. Cross over a junction and go through a pedestrian gate on to a gravel track beside the stableyards and offices. Cross over the car park, taking a path on the far side. Fork sharp right on to a narrower path right and down some steps to the Mere Pond.

4. Turn right along a water's-edge path. At the far end of this mere, cross a bridge to the left then climb between a deer fence and woodland on the National Forest Way.

5. At the top edge of the woods, leave the National Forest Way and deer fence, which forks right on a track through a gate. Instead, turn left along a track past an information panel then next right through a gate into fields. Head left along the wall and over a stile. Now cross diagonally right over two fields separated by a track and pass close to White Leys Farm. Bend right at the field end, continuing along its new left edge. After a stile, continue on the right edge of another field to the edge of some woods on the far side.

6. Turn left on to a winding track through an area of woodland and old gravel pits (now wildlife ponds). This passes several cottages and meets the A514 to the east of the village.

7. Turn left along the road and pass under the horseshoe-arched bridge. Go right at the junction with Ingleby Lane, retracing your steps to the start of the walk.

Where to eat and drink

Calke Abbey has its own restaurant, which is handily placed on the route at the Stableyard. It makes use of fresh, locally sourced ingredients where possible, and offers kids' picnics as well as a range of options from snacks to full meals.

What to see

By Ticknall's 19th-century church you can see the remains of a medieval church, St Thomas Becket's, which had become too small. The old church was so strong that it had to be blown up with gunpowder.

While you're there

Calke Abbey is in the National Forest and kids and adults alike will enjoy a visit to the Conkers adventure centre at Ashby-de-la-Zouch. Test your nerve on the high and low ropes courses, challenge yourself on the 18-stage adventure course, give the kids a messy but fun sensory experience on the barefoot walk, or experience the simulated treetops walk (watch out for the bats!).

NOTES

NOTES

NOTES

NOTES

Discover quality and friendly B&Bs

RatedTrips.com

AA